Bail Guy
Prose and Convicts

Buck Biestek c.2013

Introduction

The words, "I can, I must, and I will" – that is the way to change yourself and achieve absolute victory. - Spiritualist Paramahansa Yogananda

That simple statement is very powerful. That simple statement inspired me to author Bail Guy- Prose and Convicts.

Hanging around the local courthouses and police departments over the past thirty years, one would think that they have heard and seen it all. I can tell you that each day, there is a new angle or slant that has not been introduced yet. If I told you about some of the things I've seen and heard, you would probably think I'm nuts. I've often been told after one of my gollywomper stories, that I should write a book about it and many other tales. Well, kind of as a goof, I started to write. Before I knew it, I had put together a string of short stories that I thought were entertaining and amusing. Thus, Bail Guy - Prose and Convicts was created.

The format I chose for this project was first to introduce you to who I am and give you some background about my upbringing. Secondly, knowing a bit about what a bail bondsman is and does helps you, the reader, to understand the entire process. Finally, I wanted to share with you the experiences I've had in this real life game of Hide and Seek.

This book is dedicated to my family, friends, and all the people I've encountered along the way in my career as a bondsman.

Chapter One
Weenik's Influence

The phone rings and wakes you from a sound sleep at 12:30 A.M. You manage to answer in a groggy voice and your best friend on the other end says frantically: "I need you to bond me out! Bring down $1000 cash or call a bail bondsman. My bond is $1000.00 please get me out, PLEASE! I'll explain later, just hurry down to the police station."

You want to help your desperate friend but you don't have $1000 cash lying around. What is your next move? You call a bail bondsman. You call me, the Bail Guy.

Ahhhhh, the life of a bail bondsman. I often wake up and ask myself if I had any calls the previous night, or if I went out on a bond call last night. That is how numb a veteran bondsman becomes after years of interrupted sleep and constantly being on call in an industry that is comparable to New York City, an industry that never sleeps. Day or night, night or day, holidays, weekends, Christmas, Easter, Halloween, you get the idea. It just doesn't matter. I have to be locked and loaded and ready to go. Crimes and subsequent arrests don't have a nine-to-five schedule. People commit offenses at any given time and being in such a cut-throat, underworld business, if I don't answer the call, there are literally dozens of licensed bondmen, seemingly on every corner, who will step up and gladly steal my business. I've learned to live my life through my career, and since they are one and the same, I'm on edge every day, all day.

I guess I was destined to be a bail bondsman. From an early, and I mean early childhood, to today, I have been aware of the inner workings of bail bonds. It seems as though my entire life has been encompassed by bail bonds or the bail bond process. I grew up in a household that was bail oriented. My exposure to the industry occurred once the doctor slapped me to see if I was breathing and then continued to pummel me just for the heck of it. My Uncle Weenik was a full time bondsman and he encouraged my father to become a part time bondsman, and two of my siblings were licensed bondsmen at one time.

The Biestek Bail Bonds brand name became synonymous with bail bonds in my home town. Consequently, bail bond discussions around the house were prevalent and hearing the language and common phrases associated with bail bonds only enhanced my ability to operate as a bondsman. I have to admit, life's deck of cards dealt me a winning hand in relation to the bail industry.

I can still hear that treacherous, mundane, old rotary phone ring tone to this day. Ddddddddddnnng. Ddddddddddnnng. All of us kids would race to answer it in hopes it was Uncle Weenik asking if we would like to go for a ride to "help" him post a bond. Posting a bond is the general term used for bailing someone out of jail. It's funny; if my home phone rings now, it doesn't even faze me. It's probably some damn telemarketer that I have NO interest in wasting my oxygen supply on. Anyway, Weenik would drive over to our house and pick up any kid that wanted to go. I remember always wanting to go. I thought the whole posting of a bond process was fascinating. For "helping" Weenik we would always be given a reward afterwards. He would take us to Les' for ice cream or to Gus' for a hotdog with scrumptious chili on top. The "golden arches" at Ronnie McDonald's was also a frequent destination after posting a bond.

However, unequivocally, the greatest thrill after a bond was going for a ride in Weenik's Cessna 172 propeller airplane. He later owned a Cessna 182, so I had experience "flying in" and "flying" both models. I'll explain that last sentence later. I don't know much of the differences between the two aircrafts other than maximum speed potential, but flying around in his four seat plane was remarkable. His experience as an honorably discharged fighter pilot in WW II enabled him to continue flying until he retired from aviation in 1995. Having a personal pilot and an aircraft at the ready for sightseeing and travel was a huge asset for my extended family. Weenik would regularly take us kids up in the air just to log air time and keep his flying acuity intact. The engine on each plane also needed a minimum amount of operation to pass FAA regulations. The co-pilot flying shot gun usually was given the chance of a lifetime. Once he had established a safe air speed and altitude, Weenik would say, "Okay, you take over now." This meant we could fly the plane ourselves. Whoa, Whoa, hold your horses chief, I know what you are thinking; Uncle Weenik wasn't that crazy. His Cessna aviation device had a steering wheel and rudder on each side of the front seats. Weenik kept a vigilant eye on the co-pilot and was ready to assume the helm in the event of any emergency. There are no words to describe the adventure of flying a plane, especially as a child. (Ahem, remember "flying in" and "flying"?) Not so sure the FAA would be overly fond of this last admission and testimony of what some may consider illegal aviation. Who cares? It was all in fun right? Whatever. Weenik's white and frozen pea-green trimmed Cessna aircraft became a handy bounty hunting tool. He used it on a few bounty hunting missions, one in particular that I will discuss a bit later.

Who would have thought that the McDonald's Hamburglar, no pun intended, and flying an airplane before I had a license to drive an automobile would lead me to a career in the bail industry? Not only was I in reverence of the bail bond process and practices, but I could see that Weenik and my dad were fortunate to have a job that made people appreciative and happy. One minute I'd see a guy behind bars and the next I was walking side by side out of a jail with him. I was astonished to see how happy he was. That would be a job any kid would want to have. Of course as a young lad, I wasn't really focused on bail bonds as a career, but those subliminal bail bond messages bestowed upon me as a youngster would be awakened and mushroom in my adulthood.

My Uncle Weenik's influence was without question the key mover and shaker that really jump started my career in the industry. Weenik was the consummate, smooth- talking, debonair businessman back in his day. He was kind of like a jack of all trades and had experience in a variety of professions. He once managed a movie theatre; owned an oil company called Blue Streak, and had obviously mastered a successful bail bond operation. Furthermore, as I've mentioned, he was an accomplished pilot from World War II, and an experienced eel fisherman off the docks on the Connecticut River. If that's not enough diversity, let me mention he was a philanthropist, an avid baker, a double green-thumbed gardener, a savvy bargain hunter for "good deals," a stockholder in Ronald McDonald's famous golden arches, and a highly decorated Little League coach for Hancock's Pharmacy.

I mention the little league highlight because his brother, my FATHER, sponsored a team called "Biestek Insurance" in the same league. The strange aspect of this tidbit of information is that NONE of us Biestek children (five boys and one girl) played on "Biestek's Insurance." The boys played for my uncle on the Hancock's Pharmacy squad. That was something I could never figure out. Why the hell was I suiting up for the enemy? I was nothing but a pipsqueak, the fifth of six children in the pecking order, and wasn't smart enough or good enough to demand a trade! But we sure did enjoy playing for Uncle Weenik.

Uncle Weenik and his lovely wife Martha Lou treated us kids as their own. They didn't have any children, so we were unofficially adopted, and treated like royalty. Often, some of us kids would accompany them to exotic places for vacation. Some of those locations included Bermuda, Puerto Rico, and the Florida Keys. Day trips and weekend getaways included Boston, to see Weenik's beloved Red Sox, and Mount Snow in Vermont. They would pick up the entire tab and give us spending money to boot. One of Weenik's favorite past times was ordering our dinner for us. I'll never forget the time we vacationed in the Tarpon Springs area of Florida and I, (well, he) ordered frog legs. Out of respect, admiration, and gratitude, I couldn't say no. What a stupid choice. Ten year old kids may play with frogs, but they don't EAT them. That incident taught me a valuable lesson in life: I had to speak up for myself. Needless to say, those tiny amphibian limbs never made it into my esophagus.

On another occasion, after learning that my brother Doc was planning a trip to visit my brother Rico who was stationed in Hawaii, Weenik decided that I HAD to keep Doc company and keep an eye on him. Best of all,

Weenik paid for my entire trip. Geez, twist my arm, will you! Better yet, pinch me! Is this a dream? Before I could descend from the heavens of elation and calm down at the thought of flying to Hawaii, I was advised that the only seat available for me was in first class. Man! Did that stink!! Moreover, Weenik had allotted me spending money for a 12 day trip to our 50th state. On my flight to Los Angeles, I sat next to the saxophone player from the Bob Seger Silver Bullet Band. Close your eyes and imagine for a second, a 15 year old kid, in a first class seat on an airplane, going to Los Angeles and then on to Honolulu, sitting next to a rock and roll star saxophonist. Does it get any better than that? Who in their right frame of mind wouldn't want to be a bondsman like Uncle Weenik?

My siblings and I owe Weenik and Martha Lou oceans of gratitude. Let me briefly and informally give you the Biestek roster of children. My idiosyncrasy for using nicknames is intense and I most often use only monikers, so don't be alarmed. Heck, even my company logo has a sobriquet, Bail Guy. Rico is my oldest brother, still connected with the military and an ex-bondsman, followed by Doc, who is an optometrist. Then there's my sister Beak, a yoga guru, who is beautiful and looks nothing like a toucan. Garth, or basketball Jones (God rest his soul; his journey on this earth came to an early sunset on March 1st, 2012) was next in line and he also was a bondsman. I, Buck, am fifth on the totem pole chain of command and finally, my younger brother Jimbo rounds out the field. All of us had been involved in helping Uncle Weenik and my dad in his part time business, but only three of us followed in their footsteps.

Now that you are familiar with a bit of my childhood and my immediate family, let me explain how I was "volunteered" into a career as a Bail Bondsman. It was early spring of 1982, and I was fresh off my first year of college at Southern Connecticut State University. I was majoring in business economics and kind of trying to find my way as a young adult. Completing one year of college by no means makes anyone ready for a CEO position, but I figured I had a start in the right direction by choosing business as a major. I also had an affinity towards the field of psychology and I am fascinated by the inner workings of the mind. Believe me; I have needed expertise in both of these fields in order to deal with my client base.

The events that ultimately led to my career as a bondsman were not earth shattering. It all just kind of transpired naturally as it was meant to be. I had arrived home after finishing my delivery route for a local dry cleaning company. My uncle Weenik and Aunt Marti came over to visit (as they often did) and asked my dad, Fredju, as he was called, (remember that passion for nicknames?) if any of his kids would be interested in officially helping him with writing or posting bonds. Weenik was at the time a 65 year old, seasoned business entrepreneur who had been in the bail industry for over 15 years. By luck I happened to be hanging around the house and my father volunteered me as the chosen future assistant to Weenik in bail bonds. I didn't have a chance to say "Let me think about it" because all those childhood memories flashed before my eyes in a nanosecond: collecting cash, making people jovial, raising their gloomy spirits, being thanked for coming to the rescue, and all those magnificent treats after the bond was posted! I had an epiphany; I knew there and then that my future had bail bonds written all over it.

In June of 1982, Weenik subsidized my enrollment tuition fee in a Casualty Insurance course in Hartford. At the time, one needed to become a licensed insurance agent in the casualty field in order to get a surety bail license. The course was eight weeks long, starting in the middle of June and ending mid-August. Most of the material was a complete bore to me, even though I was interested in a business occupation. The textbook had approximately 20 chapters and only one of the chapters contained material on BONDS, more precisely bail bonds. I think it was Chapter 19 out of a total of 20. As fate would have it, I was absent the day we studied Chapter 19. It was a Tuesday and I was at the funeral of my father Fred. He had passed away on August 8, 1982 of a massive heart attack, while visiting with my brother Fred Jr. (aka Rico) in Natick, Mass.

That was one of the saddest and most shocking days of my 18 year old life. I realized that no one or nothing lasts forever and just the thought of losing my 56 year old dad broke my heart. Life would be different for this young "Buck". My entire family was in shock over losing our dad. It was tough for me to comprehend the magnitude of his death. I had to grow up in a hurry. Things were almost eerie without Dad's iron fist around to lay down the law. He was my very own E. F. Hutton because when he yelled, I listened. In fact when he yelled, the whole neighborhood listened and certainly heard him.

Being a bit addled and anxious, I thought, who would guide me as I grow in to adulthood? Who would educate me in the things 18 year old young men need to be taught? I thank the heavens for my MOM, yes MOM. She has been my shining star and will forever be. She had to wear the hat of both parents for my siblings and me. She would be the one to comfort, guide, and advise us all. The burden she overcame was tremendous. She was a widow at age 50.

Now back to Chapter 19. The instructor was very understanding and permitted me to make up the class, and I did. I then passed the mandatory Casualty Insurance exam with flying colors. On October 21, 1982 I received my appointment and license as a surety bail bond agent in the state of Connecticut.

Bail 101

Chapter Two
Bail 101

Now that you know how I became a bondsman, I'd like to offer you a quick Bail 101 tutorial on the basics of bond licenses, a bondsman's responsibilities, some personal thoughts on the problems and issues that malign the bail industry as a whole and some possible solutions to make it a proud and respected profession.

The bail bond industry has been in existence for decades in the United States. In its early days many of the laws were created from the conduct exemplified in the Wild West. Consequently, the basic principles conceived many years ago, are still widely applied and accepted today. Although time has carried on in an ever changing world, the basic premise of a bail bondsman remains intact.

There are two types of bail bond licenses in Connecticut. First is a "surety producer" license obtained through the Insurance Department and second is a "professional bondsman" license issued by the Department of Public Safety. The surety producer licensees greatly outnumber the professional licensees. The distinction between the two types of licenses is that the surety producers are backed by an appointed insurance carrier contracted with the state of Connecticut and the Professional license holder is backed by his or her own assets.

Both licenses allow for posting of bail but the big variance is that professional bondsmen tend to be a bit more judicious, for lack of a better term, in taking on a case. Many insurance producers tend to be more lax in assessing a case because their rear ends are not on the line. They have the financial backing of multimillion dollar insurance companies. The fact that this is like monopoly money to them causes some recklessness and poses a potential public safety hazard. There is a reason why some bonds are set extremely high (public safety concerns) but some insurance producers scoff at this possibility and take on very risky clients. As one would imagine, competition is fierce, which adds another level of unnecessary stress out in the field. Basically, the bail industry profit pie is being split so many ways by the influx of hundreds of licensed bondsmen that we are competing over atoms.

The role of a bondsman in the judicial system is quite complicated. Bondsmen usually hang around the courthouses and police stations soliciting for business. Currently, in Connecticut, it is illegal to solicit in or on the grounds of a courthouse. Astonishingly, solicitation is a common practice at most courthouses because there is no distinctive remedy to eradicate it. Sure the laws are on the books, but no one really knows how to enforce the laws. Even worse, no one really seems to care about bondsmen until one of us really screws up.

A bondsmen's responsibility is to guarantee that the defendant or arrestee, will appear in court on each and every date required until final sentencing. When a bail bond is executed, the bondsman is assuming liability for the amount of the bond. The bottom line is this, posting a bond puts us on the hook for the bail money. It is vital to have solid underwriting criteria to help determine a good versus bad risk bond. We never know who is going to stiff us or jump bail, so it is a constant cat and mouse type existence. When a defendant fails to appear (FTA) in court while released on a bail bond, the judge will order the bond forfeited. This means that the clock starts ticking and we have to track the defendant down and return him or her to the custody of the court. Connecticut law allows for a six month stay on the forfeiture before it has to be paid to the state Criminal Justice Department general fund. The defendant must be returned to custody within that six month time frame or the bond will have to be paid. Unless a bond company has a tree with Ben Franklins growing on it, capturing the absconder becomes a top priority.

In summation, a bondman's role within the court system is important for a few reasons. The posting of bonds alleviates some of the jail overcrowding issues. Conducting fugitive recovery captures and returning defendants to custody aids in reducing the caseload of outstanding failure to appear warrants. Judges can't judge and State's Attorneys can't prosecute without a defendant in front of them. Additionally, we are mandated to pay substantial licensing and audit fees to maintain our compliant status with the State Insurance Department and the Department of Public Safety. Finally, the bond forfeiture money that we shell out goes to the Division of Criminal Justice.

Consider this: With the stroke of a pen and for a small fee, an arrestee can be back out on the streets with the help of a bondsman before the ink on the police report pertaining to the accused's case is dry. That is some powerful stuff!

The abuse of the power that a bondsman has is a problem with the industry. Some unscrupulous bondsmen take advantage of the less fortunate and the naïve. They endear themselves to unsuspecting innocent people only to bamboozle them out of money. This is beyond shameful. The bondsmen field seems to be afflicted with unethical and uneducated men and women. I feel strongly that new agents should be required to have an Associate's degree, if not a Bachelor's degree. This essential qualification may weed out some of the jackals, who seem to thrust themselves onto the bail bond scene every few months. Passing a multiple choice exam and having adequate business and ethics training are two very different things. It may be time for the Connecticut Insurance Department to consider changes in licensing qualifications. I wish there was some mechanism to trigger proper etiquette and ethics for the agents that are desperately in need of such qualities.

The biggest vexation in the industry is greed. I know all Americans want to get their share and this is the very reason we are American. We are free to choose. I use the term free loosely; taxes, insurance, taxes, health costs, did I mention taxes?? Get the point? Greed is what causes rogue agents to cut corners, act like buzzards circling over prey, and exhibit behavior in a way that makes stomachs desire to vomit not once but twice and then upchuck again. Talk about embarrassing; at times it is unsettling to admit that certain pernicious bondsmen and I are colleagues! Yes, it is that bad….greed. That's why it is one of the big SEVEN, and I am not talking about continents.

Greed can be eliminated by taking the money out of the bondsman's hand. In other words, the defendant or someone on his behalf pays the mandated fee directly to the insurance carrier. Once the proper fee has been accepted, THEN the bondsman of choice executes the bond and is later compensated by the Insurance Carrier on a bi-weekly or monthly basis just like other licensed insurance agents in the state of Connecticut. Instead of monitoring six hundred plus agents for wrong doing, the Insurance Department would monitor about twenty five Carriers contracted to do business with Connecticut. The prospect of heavy fines and sanctions imposed upon malefactors would be a major deterrent to the greed factor.

Now that my rant about the inadequacies of bail has been unleashed on your eyes, let me tell you why I continue in this profession. As I've mentioned frequently, bail bonds have been woven into the fabric of my entire life. My personal life and business life have become one and the same. This is what I know and this is what I do. I like to say, "Just do what you do." This means: don't try to be something or someone other than who you are. Don't forget, I like to help people.

Because of how disgraceful the industry has become, I have thought about leaving this field and taking on a different   career. I've dabbled in the property and casualty side of insurance and I've been a substitute teacher. Both ventures were fulfilling, but that was not who I was. Bail is who I am and bail is what I do. I am the Bail Guy. Nothing has been as rewarding as my time as a bondsman. Bail bonds are, and always have been, in my blood.

Hoping that the industry straightens out and becomes improved through positive change keeps my nose to the grindstone. I have confidence that all the wrinkles and deficiencies in the bail bond system can and will be amended. It will take a multi-faceted joint effort among the legislators, the licensing authorities and us, the bail bondsmen.

If you, the reader, have any interest in becoming a bondsman and surviving in this industry, some innate characteristics are imperative. Having a good sense of humor is at the top of the list. You MUST have a sense of humor and make light of the darker side of crime. Otherwise, the men in the white coats will be coming for you real soon and taking you to a safe place with no sharp objects in sight. Patience and understanding are also necessary to carry on and be successful. Not everyone you meet is Jack the Ripper. I can honestly say that in my 30 plus year career, I've met only about 10 people that even Jesus Christ might say there is no hope for. God, PLEASE forgive me for that last remark. If one were to peel away the onion of an arrestee and get to his inner core, he would discover a good person at heart. However, factors such as drugs and booze trigger a myriad of offenses that under normal circumstances would lie dormant.

I have lasted this long in the bail business by being true to who I am, conducting myself in a professional and confidential manner, and having a sense of humor. Those simple key elements can never hurt in this line of work. Finally, the ability to listen to my clients and respect them for who they are has made life as a bondsman gratifying and rewarding.

I've orated enough about my opinions, haven't I? So as not to bore you into suicide contemplation, I will get off my podium and get started with our journey together.

The authentic, true-life accounts on the ensuing pages exhibit some of the predicaments I've been faced with throughout my career. I will take you to some locations such as the Caribbean, Texas, Alabama, and New York City. I will acquaint you with some interesting people I've met throughout my travels. Each main character in his or her respective story has one thing in common with the other characters I discuss. They all decided to run away from a problem. Once they opted to flee, their problem became my problem. The names, places, and some circumstances of the characters in the following chapters have been altered to protect the innocent and the guilty.

Come along with me on an emotional odyssey as I relate to you my real life games of Hide and Seek, and give you an inside look at the life of the Bail Guy.

The Missing Link

Chapter 3
The Missing Link

Chester B. was a married, middle aged, seafarer type fellow with a stepson in tow. He didn't look like your typical criminal, not that there is a universal mold for a criminal; his outward appearance was a dead ringer for the guy on Mrs. Gorton's fish sticks packages. He appeared to be a paunchy, ordinary, ho-hum, guy. Here's the "rub" (keep reading) with Chester. He was accused of making women in local department stores feel very uncomfortable by stalking them and having uninvited physical contact with them. It wasn't a onetime event with him, but a series of events that gave rise to charges of sexual assault. He had no prior arrests and had lived in the area for many years. His stepson was enrolled in the local schools and his wife co-signed the bond on his behalf.

At first glance, it seemed like a decent bond to get involved with. I know what you might be thinking: why would he get involved with a defendant with those charges? Well, in this industry one needs to have compassion and an impartial understanding of the circumstances surrounding each case, but I also have to realize that I am not dealing with "priests and nuns," as Uncle Weenik would say. In other words, I have to treat each case as a business; otherwise any one with half a conscience would not choose this enterprise as a career. As I mentioned before, most people are decent people deep down to the core.

All of the preliminary assessments of the case justified my undertaking of the $75,000 bail on behalf of Chester; he had no priors, was married with a child, had lived in the area for many years, and he had a private attorney for whom he paid a hefty retainer. Every indication pointed to Chester being a good risk. I made the decision to go forward with posting the bond – a decision that, you will learn, I regretted making.

This was my first real big bounty hunting case, but certainly not the last. It was in the mid 1980's, when I bonded out Chester. He had been attending all of his court appearances faithfully for several months and had given no indication that jumping bond was in his future.

As soon as I discovered he was a no show at court, I pulled his file and called his last known phone number. Disconnected, of course. I then phoned his place of work and that's when the iron anchor came crashing down on my skull. Chester's now ex-boss told me he had disappeared! He explained to me that Chester sold his boat called the "Old Lovely Lassie" for approximately $35,000 cash and took off. I raced down to the marina where Chester and his family were dwelling to see if what I was told was in fact true. Upon arriving I observed his boat, moored, so I stepped on board. I don't know much about boats, but I could tell that this boat, the Old Lovely Lassie, had been emptied of all its comforts and more importantly, its former inhabitants. All that was left was just a boat. I had been duped, and that feeling is worse than accidentally gulping down super strength Listerine.

Next I phoned his attorney, who disclosed to me that he suspected that Chester may have abandoned the area because HE tried to phone Chester regarding the case and received the same results as I. The attorney expressed his disappointment in his client, relating to me that he thought the case was going to end favorably for Chester. Upon completion of the call to Chester's attorney, I expressed aloud a little bit more than disappointment. Somehow I remember a diatribe replete with swear words and derogatory adjectives.

The investigation as to his whereabouts began promptly. Within a few weeks I had received a fairly reliable lead that Chester was spotted at the helm of a new boat called "Shadow Box," and was living a carefree and comfortable life in the British Virgin Islands. I had two choices: pay the bond OR go get that jerk and bring him back to where he belonged. Generally, once a defendant premeditates a plan to skip bond and then carries out that plan, my instincts tell me that he is guilty. From this point forward, I had to use every possible resource to recover my bounty. I immediately made plans to get my fanny down to the Caribbean.

I was still a young man, a couple of years removed from earning a Bachelor of Science degree. As I said, it was the mid 1980's, and at that time, the hot show on television was "Miami Vice" starring Don Johnson and Phillip Michael Thomas, more affectionately known as Sonny and Rico. I wouldn't miss an episode for anything. I loved the story lines and the music cleverly inserted at just the right time. Due to the impact Miami Vice had on me, I would assume the name of Sonny Crockett for a little bit of fun while I was on this mission.

The rumor was that Chester was hanging out on the island of Tortola. Where the hell or what the hell is Tortola? A second reliable source also reiterated and confirmed that Chester was residing in the British Virgin Islands and his boat was named "Shadow Box." What are the chances, or is this just a coincidence? Two good sources pinpointing the same general area of our massive globe was certainly encouraging. I was very confident that I would find him and return him to Connecticut. It seemed pretty simple; finding the Shadow Box would lead me to Chester the "molester." Sorry, that one was just too easy not to record.

Chester couldn't have picked a better spot to run to, because the Caribbean is heaven on earth. Crystal clear waters, easy lifestyle, honest, hardworking people. Luckily for me, I had some help in trying to locate the bond skip, my brother, Fred, dubbed Rico. Remember the influence of Miami Vice? Rico was a bit older than I, and was a veteran officer of the U.S. Army who had traveled the world extensively. He had been stationed in Massachusetts, California, North Carolina, and Kansas. Furthermore, he called Korea "home" for 2 stints, and as I mentioned, he lived in Hawaii. I describe him as an army lifer but most of us think he may be a little bit MORE involved with the government. Oh, I don't know, maybe a SPY!!!. Who's to say? Anyway, I wanted someone with his background and connections on my side.

Since there was no direct flight to Tortola, we traveled down to St. Thomas. After deplaning in Charlotte Amalie, we taxied to the boat docks and took a forty five minute ferry ride to Roadtown, Tortola. Now, never having been to the Caribbean, this volcanic island was completely "foreign" to me. It is part of the British Caribbean Island chain, which also includes one of the nicest places on earth, Virgin Gorda, and the spot to be, The Baths on Virgin Gorda. The Baths are pools of water amongst caves and rock formations that took thousands of years to develop. The exceptionally pristine aqueducts were warm and enticing. This won't be the last time you will read a description of this phenomenon.

Getting back to why I was in the Caribbean, our goal was to find the bond skip. He was a white man, middle aged, with a nautical background and a propensity to commit lewd crimes. The description I just gave of our fugitive turned out to be our biggest stumbling block; just about every sailor in and around the Roadtown, Tortola marinas, was a middle aged, white guy with nautical experience, and this made our task extremely difficult. In addition, word is that some sailors like to act outside the purview of the law, then rig their jib and hit the open waters. After I met with the local police department, Sgt. Frazier in particular, they were more than helpful in trying to locate our fugitive, for they did not want that type of person carousing around on the island.

On our first day, after de-boarding the ferry in Roadtown, we walked the short distance to what would be our living quarters for a few days, a place called the *Sea View Hotel*. It was a quaint, bed and breakfast hotel overlooking the Caribbean seaside. The proprietor was a native Tortolan woman named Ishma. She had to be in the twilight of her life, but she showed no signs of slowing down. The fountain of youth cloud must have rained down upon her. Ishma was the maid, Ishma was the bartender, Ishma was the cook, and Ishma was the waitress. Plainly, Ishma did everything. The funny thing with Ishma was, any time we wanted something, we would just open up our window or door, yell her name and she would come at our call. When we wanted to eat, we would just yell out, "Ishma!" "Ishma!" and she would yell back, "Yeaaaaaaaaaeeeehhh," and she would bring us whatever we wanted, on Caribbean time, which is a little slower paced than United States time. Months later, I would call down to the Sea View Hotel just to ask Ishma for something, anything, just to get a rise out of her. Ishma knew I was having some fun and took it in stride. Before hanging up the phone she would always thank me for calling and remembering her.

Because of the heat and distance between the Sea View Hotel and the Police Department, we decided to rent a car to avoid using the very, VERY slow public transportation. Utilizing an automobile helped us become acquainted with our new surroundings. Having a car, and driving on the opposite side of the road, mind you, was an experience all in itself. Left on red was strange, as was pulling left into a parking lot, without having to cross traffic. It took a while to get used to, especially on those twisting and turning mountainside roads that slithered throughout the island. As the Tortola skies darkened and the humid breezes abated, we decided to turn in and rest. Our search for Chester and his boat, the Shadow Box, would reconvene in a few hours.

The next morning, there was an aura of excitement and anxiety. After summoning Ishma and filling our bellies with a simple egg sandwich breakfast, we designated the rest of the day to seek and capture Chester. We spoke to local restaurateurs; we spoke to police who were helping us every step of the way, along with yachtsmen and deckhands. We showed his picture to everyone who would look at it. Although they were genuinely concerned for our benefit, no one was able to pinpoint our fugitive. No one was able to tell us that he was there or may have been there. Most of our feedback contained phrases such as, "He looks familiar," or "I might have passed him on the water," however, we received no certain or concrete evidence. Our fairly reliable tip was nothing but a tip, which ended up being a dead lead. It didn't take us long to figure out that trying to find our fugitive on the island or the surrounding islands would be like trying to find Waldo, who, if you don't know, is a character in a children's book who conveniently blends in to every crowd. Thus, finding Waldo becomes a time consuming chore!

Day two was exhausting and frustrating. We spent most of the day scouring the island, sweating our behinds off, and we were no closer to Chester or his boat. But don't feel so sorry for us; our plane didn't leave for another few days. We turned a fugitive apprehension trip into a mini vacation. Rico and I decided to see the entire island including, Pusser's Landing, Cane Garden Bay, Rhymer's Beach Bar and Grill, and visit many of the local establishments right in Roadtown, all the time keeping an eye out for our fugitive in hiding.

One restaurant in particular, had a big gathering outside at around five in the afternoon. Rico and I couldn't figure out what the commotion was all about, so we decided to follow the crowd and hang out with the locals at the indoor/outdoor restaurant in the middle of Roadtown. About five minutes after we arrived, a small pickup truck pulled up with a bed full of coconuts. The driver of the pickup, a weathered, sun spotted, old man, with a shaggy salt and pepper beard poured his thin body out from behind the wheel in an obvious drunken stupor. After straightening up as best he could, he reached back in to the cab of the pickup and clumsily removed a large machete. Once he gained control of the wavering blade, he raised it high, as though he had just slayed the dragon, totally engrossing the large mob of natives and tourists alike that had assembled at his feet. Everyone, including Rico and I, clapped and cheered. This behavior by the locals heightened our curiosity but confused us as well. We didn't know what the hell was about to happen. Rico and I had stumbled onto an authentic Roadtown Tortola happy hour. It would be nice to stumble upon Chester in the same fashion, I thought afterwards.

Next, the old man took the machete, steadied a coconut he had wrested away from its companions in the back of the truck, and in samurai fashion struck the top off of the coconut. The milky juice that had escaped during the beheading was quickly replaced with rum. The machete man repeated this process until all the nuts had been transformed into individualized pina coladas. Surprisingly, the master coconut carver was still able to count to ten using his own digits. The entire throng of onlookers participated in this island ritual. That spectacle, using one's local resources, I had never seen before, nor have I since. In addition to the coconuts, he had live Caribbean lobsters, fresh from the sea, which we all feasted on.

What an island! Being a young man and truly experiencing what this tropical island had to offer was a moment frozen in time.

It became apparent that finding Chester at this point would be equivalent to winning the Powerball, so Rico and I put our search for him on the "warm" burner and put ourselves back on the "high" burner tourist mode. Tortola was an enjoyable place to hang for a few days on a vacation, and boy did we have a vacation. With sugar white sand and aqua bays and lagoons staring us down each day, it was very difficult to take. Our journey took us to the nearby, aforementioned Virgin Gorda. Rico and I hailed a cab stationed at the landing, and asked to be taken to the Baths. This wonder of nature was about a fifteen minute ride away, on a primitive, bumpy road meandering along the serrated coast of the island. Once we arrived and were dropped off by the hack, we thought that this was the end of the world. No one in sight, just the sound of distant Caribbean waves slapping the giant rocks scattered in and around the postcard worthy lagoon.

I said to the Rasta man, "Where are the baths?"

"Dahn de paaath mahn!   You go, do naut be A-frade mahn, and you go!"

After a quick three minute walk over the sun drenched pathway to the ocean, there they were: ancient caverns of "bath" water snaking in and out of megalith rocks and boulders. The sand there was so fine it should be illegal. In order to appreciate all that the Baths offered, we had to cram our way into awkward openings among the gigantic rocks. Some entrances were only accessible by crawling, and some crevices were gained by doing the limbo. I'd bet a fancy dollar that Herve Villechaize, aka Tattoo of "Fantasy Island" fame, would have difficulties accessing some of the portals. All that hard work paid off. Hidden under the natural dome of the rocks were warm water pools, some that had never been graced with sunshine. The hollowed out recesses echoed with the sounds of gentle waves. We had discovered utopia. Ironically, if it had not been for Chester and his flight from justice, I would never have witnessed the splendors of this paradise.

The last ferry boat back to Tortola was ready to depart, so we reluctantly returned to the dock area and boarded our transportation. The scenic ride back to Tortola was majestic and upon docking at the Roadtown wharf we decided to kick back and relax. There were two reasons behind this thought process. One, we probably were not going to find Chester, and two, I was thinking about the $75,000 bond I was going to have to fork over to the State of Connecticut general fund. You read it correctly: $75,000. I hope you didn't think all my travels end in a positive note. Sometimes I get the man and sometimes the man gets me. I like to call this predicament "chasing bad money with more bad money," so let's just say the island rum was flowing and flowing and flowing. I think the damn Energizer bunny had control of the spiced rum bottle because it had an endless bottom. What the heck, it was only money.

In the evening, Rico and Sonny, to use our undercover aliases, went to the Treasure Isle Hotel, which is still there as of this writing. Just so happened that a cruise ship had moored off the island and the hot spot that the crew suggested was this particular hotel. It was a modest shelter perched upon a small hillside. Through a window behind the registration desk we could see into the deep end of the hotel pool. You'd be amazed at what goes on under water at a Caribbean bash. The party was up on the pool deck and it was crankin'. Those islanders really know how to throw a shindig. It was a night to remember, whoopin' it up in the island breezes with the steel drum band busting out 1970's rock music and ballads. Probably the finest asset of the hotel was its view of the bay which snuggled right up to road right across the street. This bay had about one hundred magnificent yachts, boats, dinghies, you name it. The strangest sight we saw was that of a man who from all appearances looked to be the missing link. I kid you not; his upper torso was that of a human being and his lower half was that of a chimpanzee. He had bowed legs with the hands/feet of a chimp. We thought it might have been the rum or a mirage, but no, this was a legitimate man /chimp. To this day I still think it may have been a hoax. Just another unique sight on Tortola that will remain with me forever.

Looking out over the bay I wondered, was Chester lying low on one of these floating residences? Did we travel all this way to throw in the towel? Did I want to lose one penny on this alleged criminal? Hell no. I just couldn't fathom giving up on this absconder. I couldn't say I gave it my best shot unless I left no stone unturned.

The following morning was the day I was first introduced to a cup of sobering coffee. Rico had come to my rescue with a large cup of java brewed by Ishma down in the hotel office. Having been around and exposed to unusual places and customs, he said coffee would set the wheels in my head back into alignment. I might never have crawled out of bed at Ishma's establishment that morning if it had not been for the caffeine fighting off a bad case of the back door "Irish Flu." God, that first cup was like nectar from the heavens. Needless to say, it was time for Ishma to fix us a nourishing scrambled eggs with toast breakfast and extra coffee for SONNY boy, and I needed an extra glass or two, maybe three, of the good old H2O to get the hydration back from all those spirits.

I was determined to go back to the police to see if they had any more information or new leads. Even though they assigned a detective to our inquiries, they had nothing new, but promised to continue their efforts in tracking down Chester.

Rico and I decided to give it one more intensive try in locating Chester by circling the entire island, stopping at the many marinas and boat launches in search of our subject, but we came up empty. We showed his picture to deckhands, locals, skippers, and everyone we passed, and we received the same response: No!, No!, And No! Exhausted and simply put, mad as a defeated rodeo bull named "The Champ," I realized that we would not be escorting Chester back to the states from this picturesque mass of earth.

Feeling better that we DID exert an all-out, last ditch effort to snag this perpetrator, Rico and I headed back to St. Thomas for our final night before boarding the 747 jumbo jet back to Connecticut. Instead of ferrying back to St.

Thomas, we decided to take a sea plane. If you have never experienced a sea plane in the Caribbean, it should definitely be on your bucket list. Not only was the view as spectacular as one could imagine, but landing on the open water was unique, to say the least. It was my one and only "water" landing. What put the icing on the cake was that the pilot didn't have to say MAY DAY! MAY DAY! as we smacked into the water with the pontoons under the wings.

The last night in St. Thomas was a bit somber because I knew we would be flying home without our quarry AND that a major dent in my bank account was imminent. I basically had come to grips with the thought of losing $75,000 over some S.O.B! I was out of options and there was no other alternative. That is the bad side of the industry. Any client is a potential loss, and if you have a weak stomach, then stick to your day job. So off we went, without our guy, back to Connecticut.

Tortola was a learning experience in many ways but at the end of it all, I had to settle the case with the State of Connecticut. The statutory stay of execution (six months) had expired and I had to meet with the State's Attorney in Middlesex County to work out a "compromise" in regards to how much I would be required to dish out. You see back then, we were able to settle cases with the state based on a wide variety of factors including documentation of our efforts to locate and return the absconder to custody, expenses incurred, how strong the State's case was against the defendant, etc. Forty-five thousand dollars was the final number. No, your eyes are not deceiving you. That bastard cost me $45,000 of my own money, out of my own pocket. DAMN!! Can you believe it? Forty-five thousand George Washingtons? I guess that is far better than having to eat the entire $75,000. I was just a young kid who after that glacier sized cold slap in the face, grew up as I was writing out the check. Damn!!. Forty-five large,forty-five big boys, forty-five whatevers!!

I have learned that every defendant is a possible headache in regards to skipping bail. It is unrealistic to think that ALL MY CLIENTS will appear in court on their assigned date

EVERY time. The reality is that many people blow off court thinking that it won't come back and bite 'em in the ass. They may be able to elude capture for some period of time, but eventually the jig is up and they are taken into custody. That is what happened to good old Chester. About three or four years after I paid the $45,000 forfeiture to the state fund (yeah you remember…$45,000…did I mention $45,000?), Chester tried to sneak back into the United States, coming from OH CANADA!, under an alias at Minneapolis Int'l Airport. I suppose I was on the right track: Chester HAD been out of the country AND had been sailing the open waters going from New York to Florida to the Caribbean. He basically traveled an obsolete Bermuda Triangle. Too bad the Triangle didn't bestow its mysterious ways upon Chester and have him come clean, turn himself in, and save me from losing forty-five large greenbacks.

As the story was related to me by law enforcement, Chester looked like a suspicious passenger at the airport and was quickly whisked into a private, secured room. The claim was that he looked like a smuggler and they wanted to question him regarding drugs. Chester gave them a false name with supporting false identification. That was a bad move on Chester's part. The unaware dumb ass gave the authorities the name of a WANTED MURDERER in Iowa. So now the heat was on and he went from a stalker whack job to a wanted murderer. Eventually, Chester convinced them that he WAS Chester, ahem… the wanted molester and not a wanted murderer. Talk about having a bad day. Do $45,000 fun tickets ring a bell? In case you were wondering, I was never able to recoup my bail money from Chester or the State of Connecticut even though Chester had been captured. I had six months to find him and I lost. Wait, back to Chester and more importantly back to JAIL for Chester. The phone call regarding his arrest that I received from Det. Mancuso of the Connecticut State Police was bittersweet. He advised me as to Chester's capture and forthcoming return to a CT jail. I was desperate to talk with Chester and I wanted him to see my countenance. I wondered how I would react when I saw him, and what I'd say to this guy. The guy that provided me a hellava good time in Tortola also created night sweats after I had to write out that damn check!

As Uncle Weenik always taught me in this business, take the high road, be above stupidity, act like a professional, praise in public and scold in private. Show little emotion and be a gentleman. The Sheriff's office was nice enough to let me visit with Chester in the local lock up at the courthouse. After his arraignment on the failure to appear, Chester and I had a little chat time together. Through our discussion I learned that Chester's wife had left him, and he lost just about everything he had except the clothes on his back. He ran out of money and friends, and his wife and stepson disowned him. Chester became a man isolated, literally, in his own prison, before he took up residence in a real prison. As strange as it sounds, I kind of felt sorry for the wretched bloke. We had a short dialogue as to what he did to remain on the lam and what I did to try to bring him back. I learned a lot from our conversation and I walked away never to look back and never to see him again. It was a surreal moment and a moment that is etched into my memory banks. Chester spent the next few years in jail and I moved forward in the bail industry having learned valuable lessons. Yep, I lost a shitload of money but just like a refined major league baseball closer, I have to have a short memory, the skin of an iguana, and the patience of Prince Harry.

As an aside, I recently traveled back to Tortola and looked up my old friend Ishma. She looked fantastic for someone who I thought was eighty, twenty-five years ago. We chatted for about fifteen minutes and spoke about how much the island had been built up and commercialized. I asked Ishma if she could fix me breakfast and she respectfully declined. I learned that Ishma retired from the hotel industry. She informed me that her daughter and grand-daughter now run the hotel and that Ishma has officially retired from cooking breakfast for her patrons as well as all of her other duties. It was great to go back and visit with my old island friends. I also went back to the "Baths" on Virgin Gorda and relished every moment relaxing amongst the shimmering fish and Jacuzzi like chambers.

Sopa de Camarones

Chapter Four
Sopa de Camarones

Carlita U. was a short, Puerto Rican woman with a heavy Spanish/English accent. She had resided in the area for several years and was well known in the community. I was familiar with some of her relatives, but I did not personally know Carlita. Unfortunately, she was arrested on suspicion of selling illegal substances. Her posse chose me to help her with her bond and I willingly obliged. She didn't fit the prototypical stereotype of a dealer, but as I mentioned before, there is not a special mold for drug dealers. She came across as ordinary, but she was below average in the easy-on-the-eyes department. In fact, directing my corneas in her direction was detrimental to my overall health. Carlita had a diminutive, stocky build and resembled a weeble wobbler. I must not and should not judge innocence or guilt based on appearance, but it is hard not to. Through the years, I have acquired a knack for assessment based solely on appearance, but at the end of the day, I just never know. I suppose

Carlita may have been guilty since she decided to split town before her appearance date and took off to parts unknown, at least temporarily parts unknown.

After receiving the bond forfeiture notification from the court (this time the bond was $20,000), the wheels were set in motion to locate Carlita and bring her back to the jurisdiction to face the judge. Carlita's co-signer on the bond was an acquaintance of hers, who was also one of her customers. Since the time he signed for her and the date of the F.T.A., he had lost his job and had no source of legal income. Basically, as my friend Bradley likes to say, "He didn't have a pot to piss in or a window to throw it out of." I canvassed the neighborhood asking questions, talking to neighbors, family, and friends. Amazingly, more than one family member was very willing to rat her out and support me in my pressing endeavor. My guess is that she either pissed them off, ripped them off, or both.

Remember Uncle Weenik's credo? Be respectful, treat people fairly, take the high road etc.? Well, that is the tact I employed. Getting information is much easier using the good guy approach. I am not always met with open arms when asking for assistance or leads, so exercising the hat in hand style is most efficient. After about a week of dogged investigation, I found out her location, Yabucoa, Puerto Rico. It was fairly predictable that Carlita would flee to Puerto Rico; she was a native of Puerto Rico and still had family ties there. Common sense told me she had packed her belongings and headed back to her place of birth. What better place to escape, she may have thought. In Puerto Rico, Carlita would be welcomed, safe, hidden, and she probably thought I would not spend the time or money going to Puerto Rico and bringing her back. Carlita underestimated my will NOT to lose $20,000, due to her negligent behavior.

My first thought on trying to catch Carlita was to see if I had any hooks in Puerto Rico. "Hook" is slang for connection, not for the famous captain. Rico, the army lifer that assisted in my efforts to locate Chester, immediately entered my brain. Rico logged more miles pounding the proverbial pavement than William" Willy" Loman did in "Death of a Salesman". Rico's nomadic military life afforded him many contacts throughout the world. Rico HAD to know someone; he just had to. I was accurate in my supposition. It just happened that Rico had some pull down in Puerto Rico, an army buddy stationed at Fort Buchanan in San Juan. I HAVE to use a fictitious name for this guy, because if the army finds out what he did to help us, he might be dishonorably discharged or lose his pension, if he's already said adios to Uncle Sam's regime. I'll call him Albert.

I sent Albert a picture of Carlita via USPS and within about two days of receiving her mug shot, he called and said, "I've got her," in a heavy Spanish accent.

I said, "What? Got her?"

"Si si, got her". Albert replied.

This response included Spanish and English. However, understanding Albert's speech was like understanding quantum mechanics. Rico never mentioned a possible language barrier the size of the Grand Canyon.

"Do you have her with you NOW?" I earnestly inquired.

"No, but I know her live!" He replied in yet a third variation of what he passed off as English.

It was December and I was more than happy to get out of Dodge and bring Carlita back as my very own Christmas present to the waiting arresting authorities. My gift to Carlita would be a one way ticket from Puerto Rico back to the mainland. Rico was overseas at the time, so I enlisted my younger brother Jimbo, to join me on this particular mission. He was available to assist because he had just completed his Master's of Business program at Boston College and had a few days before he would have to embark on his new sales position with a national company. Jimbo was a towering, athletic young man who had recently spent the previous four years of his life getting an education and playing Division I football at Boston College. He stood six feet five inches and weighed close to two hundred seventy pounds, a perfect combination for a defensive end, which was his position, and to have as a backup. I felt confident that if Carlita tried to run, she would not have been able to escape.

While I'm bragging about Jimbo's athletic prowess, I must also mention my older brother Garth, God rest his soul, who also played football at BC. His solid play as fullback blocking for the likes of, hmm, Heisman trophy winner Doug Flutie, led him to being drafted by the Denver Gold of the United States Football League.

I was the kid sandwiched in the middle of those two scholar athletes. I was no slouch mind you, coming in at six feet two inches and carrying around two hundred fifteen pounds, but football was not my forte.

This trip to Puerto Rico would be my first extended trip to the island. I actually had touched down just long enough for a cup of coffee on my way back from the failed Chester the molester fiasco. So technically, it was my second time in San Juan, but my first time seeing more than the interior of the airport. Thankfully, I had taken Spanish both in high school and college so I was able to converse somewhat with the natives. It is amazing how quickly I remembered the language once I was thrust in to a situation where I HAD to speak it. The islanders got a kick out of the way I massacred the tenses and gender endings of the words. My Spanish speaking skills were by no means perfect, but charmingly effective. By comparison, it was no different than a predominantly Spanish speaking person "habla-ing" English. In fact, I still integrate and practice Spanish frequently. Apparently all those tests and essays DO come in handy. It helped that in one of my college Spanish classes, I spoke only Spanish during the entire class. Not one word in English came out of my mouth the whole semester. For that little psychological apple for my teacher, I received an "A". I guess it was part of my training in schmoozing. How ironic. I wasn't that fluent in Spanish, but just for my efforts and keeping the theme of the course, "Conversational Spanish," I was justly rewarded.

When Jimbo and I landed, we went through the hassle of getting our luggage and proceeded to go outside in search of Albert. Luckily for us, Albert created a sign reading "Biestek

Boys" that he was waving over his head like an inverted pendulum. He was also jumping up and down like a kangaroo. Ray Charles would not have missed Albert or his shenanigan greeting. Rico had described Albert as a smooth and persuasive, thirty- something, Puerto Rican native who was built like a prize fighter. Now, I had never met Albert, nor had Jimbo, but when Rico said he's Good People, it is understood that he is GOOD PEOPLE. I can't say enough about the old adage, it's not what you know, it is WHO you know. We asked him if he was indeed Albert, and he assured us with a "Si si, venga venga"! This translates to yes yes, come come. We hopped into his car and Albert started spewing out Spanish that sounded like some massive run-on sentence for all of eternity as he drove away from San Juan International Airport. Jimbo and I looked at each other with a perplexed look, as if to say WTF is he saying. As we sat motionless and speechless, Albert continued on for about another minute, and then clammed up his yapper. I was thinking to myself, is he done? More pertinent, what on God's creation did this hombre say? Then, nothing but dead silence except for the radio bubbling out a rendition of "Guantanamera." Suddenly, Albert broke into a laugh that would curl the hair of Yul Brenner as Ramses in the Ten Commandments.

"Hey Buck, Jimbo, how are you guys? It is my pleasure to meet you. Rico has told me all about you."

We were stunned to hear Albert speak impeccable English. At that moment I knew Albert and I would get along just fine because we both had a strange sense of humor. He was a prankster and I was up for the challenge. Although laughter is a precursor for putting people at ease, I was on high alert; carefully interpreting Albert's every utterance. I had to deem what was factual and what was total bullshit. Don't forget we were hanging out with a total stranger in a place we had never been to and HE was our guide and transportation. Sometimes I have to let my gut instincts dictate my decisions and I must admit, Albert was a master jokester to the point of making me feel uneasy. I sensed that Jimbo felt the same way.

All I could do at this point was have faith in Rico's recommendation.

Albert treated us to lunch at his favorite bodega. I felt like I was with Uncle Weenik because Albert ordered for us. By the way, his choice for us, rice and beans, was delicious. This was a nice gesture on his part. He must have known that we would DEFINITELY catch Carlita and he would be handsomely compensated for his assistance. Naturally, a small almuerzo (lunch) on his tab was chicken scratch compared to the cash that would vanish from my pocket and find a resting place in his wallet. Afterwards, he brought us to our inexpensive hotel for an uneventful check in. Albert said to take it easy because he had set up dinner for us that evening at Juanita's.

Out of the company of Albert, Jimbo and I discussed our strategy to apprehend Carlita. We were still not sure about him at this point, so we had to formulate a backup plan if Albert didn't come through. I hoped my faith in brother Rico's recommendation would overrule my doubts as to Albert's sincerity, since he was hard to read and constantly joking.

At dinner, we would further discuss capturing Carlita, and our safe return to Connecticut. When I am on a mission, particularly on an island with limited modes of exiting, such as Puerto Rico, timing is everything. We had set plans to return on a date certain with a one way ticket for Carlita, so it was paramount that we try to time the capture with jetting out of town. Unfortunately, sometimes the timing is off and I have to ad lib my next move. Albert was confident he knew where Carlita was and that it would not be a problem getting her. Albert failed to mention that we would be transformed into "bounty sitters" for an extended time period. "Don't worry" Albert assured us. "This will not be a problem".

Albert picked us up later in the day and we headed over to Juanita's. Jimbo and I had thought Juanita's was a restaurant, but Albert drove us to a shanty, rundown neighborhood with no eatery in sight and parked his car. Was this another gimmick employed by Albert? Was he kidding around?

No, we WERE at Juanita's. As we exited the car, I couldn't help but be a bit concerned. Where the hell was he taking us? Albert urged us to follow him and we obeyed. Juanita's home was quite plain in appearance from the street. We made our way through her postage stamp sized yard to the front stoop. The yard had one lone palm tree and bamboo stalks close to her front door. Before we could knock, the door swung open and there stood Juanita. She was in her mid-thirties, stout, and had a face lined by the Caribbean sun. Juanita spoke no English: solamente espanol! Juanita ushered us in and gave us a hug like we were long lost relatives. She extended her arm out like a salesman showing off a prized product and urged us to sit down. Welcoming and inviting are two mainstays in Puerto Rican tradition. It was apparent that Juanita was proud of her heritage. She went out of her way to make our visit to her modest home memorable because that's what proud Puerto Ricans do. Since we had never been to Puerto Rico, she wanted to make us feel like family.

Once we were situated on the divan and chairs, we were given an adult beverage. Not sure what the hell it was, but it tasted cold and sweet, so I sat back and enjoyed a welcome cocktail. I was thinking I could get used to this kind of treatment! The aroma that escaped from the kitchen's stove was cilia scintillating and savory. If Jimmy Durante was with us, he probably would have passed out inhaling such fine scents with his big ol' schnozz. Juanita had prepared a feast of rice and beans, pork, plantains, and her specialty- sopa de camarones, shrimp soup. Salsa music blared throughout the home which made it hard to talk without using my entire larynx. We were basically shouting out our conversation, but the sapid food and pungent aromas took precedence over the cacophony.

Juanita's home was a small, four room place with little décor and a lavatory that Walter Hudson would never be able to fit into, let alone an average sized person. For informational purposes, Mr. Hudson may have been the largest human since the invention of the bathroom scale. But, at that time, it was our personal restaurant with our own personal chef, Juanita. Her hospitality was exceptional and her dinner menu was peerless. Juanita waited on us like we were kings and was happy to do so. I guess Albert had some great connections of his own. To this day I'm not sure if Juanita was a relative, friend, or girlfriend of Albert's. It didn't matter anyway. He hooked us up in a big way. So much for my earlier apprehension when I first arrived, huh? I could not have felt more comfortable as a guest in Juanita's home.

We dined and relaxed for a few hours and went over our capture plan for Carlita. The plan was basic: find Carlita and bring her back to Connecticut. According to Albert, he had canvassed the area where Carlita was living and reported to us that danger was of minimal concern. I had to trust him. He was the trained military guy and I was the younger brother of his friend, Rico.

Carlita lived at least an hour away from San Juan and we wanted to get her early in the morning. In fact, morning is the best time to capture bail jumpers, when they are half asleep, unsuspecting, and less of a threat to scamper, especially in sleepwear, or lack thereof. The blueprint was set and the next day we would drive to Yabucoa in anticipation that she would be there. All of our plans were based upon Albert's assurance of Carlita being in a certain abode. I had reservations because Albert seemed too relaxed. Jimbo and I were tense and hyped up thinking about the capture. I was thinking Albert had BETTER be for real. One of my pet peeves is chasing bad money with more bad money, so I hoped that this particular mission would not fail me.

Morning came earlier than expected, if that is even possible, and we were once again with Albert. He drove us out of San Juan through Caguas on our way to the southeast corner of Puerto Rico, to a small, sleepy hamlet called Yabucoa. Albert entertained us the entire way with Army stories about adventures he and brother Rico had experienced. He had us peeing our pants with his sense of humor, but at the same time, he was dead serious about our mission. He would shift gears in relation to his stories and our mission more than a speeding semi trying to make an unanticipated stop.

Although I had my doubts, Albert exemplified a valuable characteristic of a dedicated soldier; he was exceptionally focused on our fugitive apprehension cause. I was finally convinced that Albert was rock solid, and felt like an idiot for not coming to this conclusion earlier. As I mentioned before, Albert was "good people," but I wouldn't want to cross him. I think he was a highly trained combat officer and probably could have taken us both out in a matter of seconds. Obviously it was good to have him on OUR side during this recon mission.

The three of us meandered our way along and happened to pass by the Lifesaver Candy Company between San Juan and Yabucoa. No bull, we smelled the particular flavors of those candies in the air, lime, orange, cherry. The bouquet was incredible and it also rivaled the smell of Juanita's fine cooking. Further along, we drove through a portion of a rain forest which was quite magnificent, with its lush greenery and natural fruits.

Looking back, I was overwhelmed by the experience. Every moment was a virgin encounter. Enough of the sensitive side of my psyche, we had a mission to accomplish and SHE was only about fifteen minutes away from our grasp.

We pulled up to what appeared to be a mini-housing project on a rolling hillside. A smattering of people dotted the dusty pathways leading to and from each apartment. Young children happily kicked a ball around while they giggled incessantly. We decided to survey the area from Albert's SUV and look for any possible peril. Albert pointed out Carlita's apartment in the middle of a rectangular edifice. He was confident that she was residing there.

We all sat there for a brief time, unnoticed and discreet, in stakeout mode and assessed the situation. There had to be another exit around the other side of the building, so Jimbo was assigned that post. The sun-bleached, sea gull spattered, cinder block building was two stories high, with about ten units per story, and Carlita's was almost dead center in the alignment of doors. We took a deep breath and contemplated any possible danger that could be in store for us. Did she have a gun? Would she use it? Hey, if she got caught, she would go to prison. Was she crazy or desperate enough to fire upon us to avoid capture? Were there any other potential dangerous people in her apartment? Would the innocent children at play be in harm's way? I cannot speak for Jimbo or Albert, but my heart rate dramatically increased. I felt the pounding in my thorax and my temples. I was definitely pumped up by the thrill of the chase. The unknown is an adrenaline precipitator. I had to be prepared for anything to effectuate a smooth and safe capture.

Just before we exited the SUV, Carlita's front door opened. A woman who fit Carlita's description laboriously exited the entrance way lugging a clothesbasket, and proceeded to amble down the three step drop to her very own dusty path. The woman abruptly dropped her heavy basket and inhaled violently to catch her breath. Standing there with wet laundry ready to be hung on a makeshift clothesline was Carlita. The time was about 9:30 A.M., and it was time for us to react. Albert and I leisurely strolled up the path while carrying on a fake conversation, in "espanol" mind you, never taking our eyes off of her. Jimbo started around the back of the building but didn't get too far. We had approached Carlita and she was shocked to see my face.

"Carlita! You remember me?"

"Yeah…?" She replied in a befuddled and somber tone.

"Carlita, it's time for us to go back to Connecticut." I told her.

Without hesitation, she eyeballed the clean wet clothes and said, "Let's go." No, I thought, it can't be this easy, can it? She didn't even want to hang out her clothes to dry? How inconsiderate was that?

I asked her if she wanted to pack a bag to bring back with her or if she needed to do anything as far as her living arrangements, but she declined. She knew her time on the run had expired. So off we went, back to San Juan with Carlita. Unfortunately, I had a major hurdle to overcome; our flight didn't leave until the next day and we needed a place to keep her until then. We couldn't drop her off at the local jail because there was not a valid extradition hold on file for her in Puerto Rico. Not surprisingly to me, Connecticut would only extradite her from a surrounding state. Once again, Albert said this wouldn't be a problem. As he drove, I interrogated Carlita and eased her troubled mind. I assured her that everything would be okay. For understandable reasons, Carlita was concerned about what was going to happen to her back in Connecticut, how much jail time was in her future, and how her life would drastically change being in prison. That was a HER problem, not a ME problem.

To have connections while plying this trade is definitely an asset. Albert drove directly to Fort Buchanan military base and set us up in one of the barracks. How he was able to do this was incredible. Jimbo and I didn't have clearance on the base and certainly Carlita DID NOT have clearance to be on the base. Somehow, because of Albert's military status, we passed the guard at the gate and proceeded to our new "hotel room" within the confines of Fort Buchanan. Albert must have had the biggest juice card possible to pull this stunt off. Not only did he get us in under the detection of the guards, but back out for dinner, with

Carlita. As I said, we treated her with respect and dignity. We even eventually took her cuffs off and allowed her free movement within our area of the barracks and while we were out to dinner that evening. I guess you could say that she was our prisoner/dinner date. Someone was always within arm's length of her. It didn't take Carlita long to figure out she could trust us with her life, besides, she had no choice. She was our responsibility until we arrived back to a Connecticut jail. SAFELY!

For our overnight stay at hotel Fort Buchanan we had both exits blocked with recliners. The front and back doors were the only way to get out. It was like a New Orleans shotgun home set up. The two bedroom doors were locked so entrance was impossible. Albert somehow figured this out ahead of time. In fact Albert was quick on his feet and could adapt to any situation with ease. Albert was the epitome of a bail enforcement agent. I guarded the fort, no pun intended, while Jimbo caught some zees and vice versa. Incredibly, Carlita didn't make a move to escape and slept the whole night through on a couch nearby.

As a new day dawned, Carlita knew this would be her last day of real freedom for a while. She was facing at least five years in Niantic prison for failure to appear, notwithstanding the original drug charges she faced. She was going back to a new home away from home, so to speak.

We all piled into Albert's SUV and headed back to San Juan International Airport. I was glad to be leaving because I didn't want to spend another night like a lookout soldier on the front lines. I say that tongue in cheek, so please forgive me, you, the men and women who protect my very freedom.

By this time, Carlita was treated more like a traveling companion than a prisoner. All this was prior to 9/11, so getting through security and boarding the plane were much easier than today. We notified security, with the help of Albert's penchant to be a smooth talker, as to the purpose of our travels. Honestly, I don't think security really cared who we were, or what we were doing, as long as we were leaving without incident. And we did just that. Albert walked us up to the gate which was permissible back then, and we said our respective adios'. I also thanked Albert for all his help and without further delay I handed over his commission. Albert smirked childishly and shook my one hand with both of his. It was evident that he realized I had given him a beefy tip (once again I must apologize for the humor) because he kept repeating gracias over and over and over. Carlita, Jimbo, and I scurried down the jet way as Albert's one hundredth gracias exited his mouth. By the time I reached the door to the jet, Albert's voice had become an indiscernible whisper.

During the flight, as I spoke to Carlita, I sensed that she was remorsefully aware of the cold reality that faced her. The closer we got to JFK, Carlita's good spirits diminished. Her attitude was poor and she was visibly upset. She was not on her way to a picnic, but to state prison for a few years.

We landed safely and walked to our snow covered car. There had been a storm in the NYC area a day or two earlier and the parking lot was slick and slushy. Poor Carlita was dressed in a sleeveless dress with flip flops. I had given her the opportunity to pack a bag, but she had declined. Now she wished she had brought a coat and shoes. Lucky for her, I had an extra sweatshirt in my car and she immediately put it on. The drive back to the jail intake center was tedious and yawn evoking, as Carlita didn't utter one word. She was "hit," as they say on the street. The entire drive home, I played the Neil Diamond song "Coming to America". I thought that ditty was appropriate for this circumstance. She was turned over to the police and I saved myself $20,000. Not only that, I was wined and dined red carpet style with some new found friends, and I had an opportunity to see and smell some of the natural beauty of Puerto Rico. Not a bad couple of days work.

Western Union Rendezvous

Chapter Five
Western Union Rendezvous

Roxanne Y. was a local resident who was just trying to make a living for herself and her daughter. She and her common law husband Miguel were an odd looking couple by normal standards; she stood about 5'-10" and he was about 5'-2". They had both been involved with petty crimes for a few years, and over that time they had built a professional relationship with me. I wrote a few bonds for them and they ALWAYS appeared in court. But then, the stakes increased dramatically when Roxanne was arrested for prostituting her daughter. Roxanne would be facing some serious prison time (up to twenty years) for risk of injury to a minor. The allegation was that she was prostituting her teenage daughter out for her personal wealth. Basically, she was a mother pimp, but her own daughter? Her own flesh and blood? It is almost unthinkable. I am not suggesting that if it was someone else's daughter it would be okay, but one's own daughter is uncommon. As a result of this arrest, she decided not to stick around to see the results. Roxanne disappeared faster than the last piece of good old Grandma's pumpkin pie on Thanksgiving night. Now I was on the hook for $12,000 and pretty ticked off. Here we go again; a battle of wills was in motion. I wasn't going to let this lady stiff me for some substantial coinage.

Luckily I had a pretty solid co-signer for Roxanne. His name was Henry and he was an elderly man with an obvious hearing impediment. His speech was very difficult to understand and it took several "what's?" for it to register. Upon learning of her disappearance, I immediately contacted Henry and advised him of his potential liability if Roxanne did not come back to face the music. Henry, as well as any other co-signer on a bond, had been screened carefully and thoroughly questioned. It is my responsibility to make them aware of the possible financial onus if the person they are signing for flees. I make it a point to go over the responsibility and liability they are undertaking. In my humble opinion, the co-signer is probably more important than the defendant, in terms of protecting my financial exposure.

Henry didn't take the news well and started on a three minute curse-laden tirade with words that would have made a monk faint. As he was popping' off one F-bomb after another with a few more choice words, I couldn't help but be quite amused. Here was this guy who could be my grandfather swearing like a drunk Hillbilly on his 10th birthday. Sorry West Virginia for that one, but I couldn't resist. Even though he had a pronounced speech AND hearing disability, he was quite adept at cursing and his choice of swear words would have impressed comedian Katt Williams.

Now, Henry and I became allies with one common goal, get Roxanne. We both had a dog in the fight. Henry knew that if Roxanne didn't return he would have to pay me. I knew that if Henry suddenly "lost his wallet" or claimed to have "short pockets," then I'd have to pay the state and try to recoup my losses from him. It was a tightrope walking situation between us, and had to be dealt with like a swollen ankle, gingerly. Henry vowed to get that b%t#% one way or the other.

After a few weeks, Roxanne contacted Henry and he, in turn, immediately contacted me. She didn't tell him where or who she was with, but did call to apologize about sticking him for the bond and promised to pay him back. When I found out this morsel of information, it was evident that she and her common law hubby Miguel had no intention of returning, EVER! Between the two of them they didn't have two nickels to rub together.

I kept a close vigil with Henry, who had been having regular contact with Roxanne. It was a strange relationship between them. Maybe their closeness was based upon Roxanne pimping out her daughter. I'm not accusing him of having an illicit relationship with the daughter, because I don't know one way or the other, but it was definitely a weird combo. How Roxanne and Miguel finagled this elderly man into signing for Roxanne was a mystery. In my mind, Miguel was just as guilty, but he was never officially charged.

During Roxanne's next call to Henry, she divulged to him that she, Miguel, and her daughter were in the Williamsburg section of Brooklyn, NY. Roxanne was desperate and asking for money. Her funds had run stone cold dry, and I suspected they resorted to more petty crimes such as theft, panhandling, and "chew and screw," (which occurs when someone orders a meal at a restaurant, eats it, then leaves without paying for it). This crime is one of the oldest in the book of crimes. Living by these means must have taken a toll on them. Besides, if they were caught and formally identified, she would have been held for Connecticut authorities to come take her back. So the sobbing emotional boo hoos came cascading down onto Henry like Niagara Falls. Henry promptly informed me of this latest development and with the help of local police here in Connecticut, we hatched a plan for her capture and return to jail. The cops and the court wanted her as much as I did, due to the nature of her offense.

Roxanne called every Thursday and asked for money from Henry, and he would oblige her with small amounts to gain her trust. Henry would wire the money to her. That was the turning point in the case. We tracked the Western Union pick up station to a location on Grand Street in Little Havana, Brooklyn. The hunt was on. The following Thursday would be her last day of freedom for a while, but she didn't know it, although she must have known her life on the run would not last forever. She called Henry at her usual 8:00 A.M. time and he said the money would be available by 1:30 P.M.

For this trip, I hired the services of a female bounty hunter named Natalie. I knew her from a local law enforcement agency in my area and she was the perfect and consummate professional agent. She had the unique ability to calm down dramatic and volatile situations with the power of reasoning. She didn't look tough, in fact she could have made a living as a model, but she was gritty and strong willed with a knack for compassion and understanding. I also needed a member of the opposite sex to handle any possible confrontational contact. It would not be appropriate for me to give a female bond jumper a smack down. In hindsight, I should have brought female help when I apprehended Carlita in Puerto Rico. I needed Natalie to do the pat down and handling of Roxanne if we captured her. Natalie was trained to search for needles, drugs, and weapons. Roxanne could have had all three on her or none of the above. That is what makes this part of the job exhilarating and dangerous, the unknown. I also needed Natalie to act as decoy, because Roxanne knew me and could spot me from at least a city block away.

A local news reporter who had been following Roxanne's case found out I was going to Brooklyn and asked to accompany me. After some serious thought, I decided to take her with me. A little free publicity never could hurt, right? Especially if she saw me demonstrate what I preach: treat people with respect and dignity and act like a true professional, which is exactly what I do anyway, reporter present or not. I advised the reporter to be careful and stay at a safe distance to avoid any problems that might arise. On the way down to Brooklyn, the reporter interviewed Natalie and me ad nauseam. She wanted to know all about the industry and how it works. She grilled Natalie and me for the hour plus trip, but as we crossed the Williamsburg Bridge, a silence fell upon my minivan. It was time for us to get serious.

We located the local precinct to let them know our purpose for being in the area. It is vital, as well as mandated, to notify local authorities as to why we are in their jurisdiction, and what our intentions are. Let's just say that Brooklyn, NY and Meriden, CT are nothing alike. We finally found a parking spot after about twenty minutes of searching. I anticipated parking in a spot close to the Western Union station. I didn't want to walk a prisoner down a street in Little Havana any further than necessary. This was not my turf. A stranger in a strange town, I was trying to keep under the radar. Neither Natalie nor I blended in with the locals, because we did not look Cuban, however, that didn't thwart our mission. Ironically, the reporter did look like she could have lived there.

We arrived around noon time and the adrenaline was spewing like ashes at Mount St. Helens. Our vantage point was in an unusually small Cuban café diagonally across the street from the Western Union outlet, about fifty man-size paces from our spot. We ordered some espressos, sat, and waited. And waited…and waited… and talked about nothing. I stared intently at the entrance to the Western Union and chimed in occasionally on our conversation about nothing. It was a surreal Seinfeld situation. Let me proclaim, sitting and waiting is nerve racking. I wondered if she would be dumb enough to reveal her location and actually show up. Would Miguel be with her? Worse yet, would her teenage daughter be with her? Could someone else be with her? As we sat and watched, all these scenarios played out in my head, one after another. We were prepared and ready for everything. My theory is that if I expect the worst then anything less will be relatively easy to handle.

At 1:30 P.M., as fate would have it, Roxanne and Miguel walked down the street across from us with their eyes affixed to the entrance door to Western Union. Their steady gaze at the business front rivaled that of Mr. Cheswick and the other lunatics eyeballing Randle P. McMurphy after he had been given an involuntary shock treatment in the all- time classic movie, <u>One Flew Over the Cuckoo's Nest</u>. Both Roxanne and Miguel looked disheveled and seemed to have been living as though they had no shelter. Even though I was zeroed in on them like a cheetah on a dinner mission, I couldn't help but notice they really looked desperate and downtrodden. They both entered the store and we quickly exited the café, and arrived at the front door of the Western Union within fifteen seconds. Natalie, the reporter, and I walked in like soldiers and approached the couple who, by this time, were waiting in a line of about five people.

"Roxanne!" I said loudly.

Roxanne turned around and almost fainted. The look on her face was like a MasterCard advertisement, priceless. She most definitely recognized me. Miguel quickly turned around and saw me as well and just about flipped his lid. He was dumbfounded. While this eye exchange took place, I peripherally noticed Natalie had Roxanne jacked up against the wall, gently placing handcuffs on her. I explained to the manager that she was wanted in Connecticut for a felony FTA and we were taking her back immediately. The customers in the store didn't even flinch as this was going on. I got the impression that this wasn't the first time they had witnessed an arrest taking place in the neighborhood. Without further ado, we proceeded out of Western Union, down Grand St. to my car parked a block away. Astonishingly, it was right where I had left it, with all four tires still on it!

Miguel and Roxanne begged us to let her go. They promised me she would be there Monday to turn herself in to authorities, but I wasn't having any of that BS. Furthermore, Miguel was whining like a bratty two year old about wanting a ride back to Connecticut with us! I tersely snapped at him and said, "That ain't happening!!" I may look dumb but I ain't stupid. No way was I letting this guy drive back with us. NO! Absolutely not. I had to be firm but also respectful to them. As I mentioned, they did not look well, and it was obvious they had been living hand to mouth recently. Miguel again pleaded with me for a ride just before we loaded up into the minivan, and I explained to him in no uncertain terms, he would NOT be coming back with us. We did allow the couple one last embrace and then the door closed with our fugitive safely secured. As we drove away, Miguel was running parallel to us down the street like he was saying goodbye to someone leaving on a train and he was on the boarding platform.

As I looked in my rear view mirror, Miguel eventually disappeared into the crowded streets and we were on our way back to Connecticut without any major problems. Upon arriving at the police department, we turned Roxanne over to be officially booked for the felony FTA. My next move was to call Henry and thank him for his cooperation. He was ecstatic that she was back, and that he was no longer liable to me for the $12,000. It was a win-win situation for both of us.

The only loser, as always, was the absconder. Roxanne spent the next couple of years behind bars at the state prison for women. I am not quite sure whatever became of Miguel and the center of the issue, the daughter.

Think Like A Bail Jumper

Chapter Six
Think like A Bail Jumper

Willie T. was a quiet, stocky, clean-cut Hispanic fella with the world at his feet. He lived in a modest trailer home, had a decent job, and he did not have a wife or kids to go home to. Willie considered himself somewhat of a ladies man. He had a lot of party time at his disposal and that was his demise; Willie turned into a drug dealer and also a drug user, and that is a bad combination. As fast as the money came in, it went out or up in smoke. To no one's surprise, Willie found himself in the back of a police cruiser on his way to the jail house. Willie was booked, arraigned and subsequently bonded out by yours truly. His bail was set at $50,000.00 and a friend of his quickly forked over the mandated fee and co-signed on behalf of Willie.

Willie seemed like a good risk. He had a minor record and a good private attorney with an impeccable reputation. He also owned that trailer home which was in decent shape. His chances of doing a long jail bid were minimal, except for the fact that he was on probation for a prior offense at the time of his drug sale arrest. Before long that probation warrant was signed and served on Willie while he was appearing in court. Once again Willie called upon me to post his new bail in the amount of $15,000. After weighing all the factors, including the now increased risk, I posted bond and Willie was free. He appeared as required for a few court dates and then agreed to a sentence. The execution of the sentence was stayed so Willie could get his affairs in order. This is a common practice with many courts in Connecticut. Then the shit hit the fan; Willie was a no show at his sentencing. Both bonds were ordered forfeited by the judge. Willie was on the loose and I needed to track him down. Thinking about losing $65,000 was enough to keep me sleepless for many a night.

I immediately looked at his file and started the chase. His attorney hadn't heard from him. His co-signer hadn't heard from him. I must mention that his co-signer told me to go to hell when I told him he owed me $65,000.00. I thought silently, "What a piece of fecal matter!"

Willie hadn't been seen on the streets by his dope customers. It appeared that Willie had vanished into thin air. He quit his job, which didn't surprise me. He had the decency to tell his boss he was "going away" for a little vacation, but didn't have the decency to follow through with his promise to the court. I can tell you that judges don't take kindly to defendants that plead for time to get their shit straight before their bid, and then blow off court. This judge was maaaaaaaaaaaad! As a wet hen. I was mad as two wet hens; I had to chase down a $65,000 absconder.

For the next few weeks I worked this case like a crazed animal. I had lost some major frog skins earlier in my career. Remember Chester the molester? I was definitely hot to get this kid. Every lead I followed came up cold. Word was he was in Puerto Rico. I thought probably not, since he had no family there, as far as I knew. Then I heard utterings he was in New York City. Maybe, anyone can get lost for a while in NYC. Then some semi-concrete information came regarding Florida. Word had it that he had an ex-wife living in the Holly Hill section of Daytona Beach. I called and spoke to her and she claimed he had not been there. In fact she was adamant about him NOT being there and proceeded to verbally abase him like a Hatfield would a McCoy. This interested me because most people would not take it to that extreme, so I thought there might be some truth in the rumor that he was hiding in Florida. I spoke to her on several occasions and every time she denied knowing where he was. If he REALLY wasn't there, then why did she answer my calls? Why did she return my calls? Perversely, this really had me believing he WAS there.

Remember, having connections is always a good thing. As luck would have it one of my police buddies had a "hook" in the post office in Daytona Beach. We sent down Willie's picture and a description that included some obvious and unmistakable tattoos. The hook was going to do some drive-bys and alert the mail carrier to be on the lookout for Willie. Within days we had some positive feedback, but it wasn't enough for me to go on a wild goose chase like I did in Tortola. I needed proof positive that Willie was back with his ex and keeping a low profile. The mailman claimed that a red Ford Mustang he hadn't ever seen before was parked at the ex-wife's house. Damn! Was this just a coincidence? The car had no plates on it, so we couldn't trace it. Had she bought a new car for Willie?

I decided to use the services of a bounty hunting organization based out of Aiken, South Carolina. This organization had a solid reputation and had been referred to me by a trusted colleague. I signed a contract with them, mailed Willie's file to them and they were going to drive down and check it out. They would be paid for their services only if they captured Willie. Not a bad set up. I didn't have to spend time AND money on a "possibility." I could use these guys and stay put. I was trying to be proactive but frugal with my expenses. I didn't want to be a Stanley Steamer (a person who thinks a double or nothing bet is a good bet) and chase bad money with more bad money. I would gladly pay top dollar to them if they were able to retrieve Willie. So I waited…and waited and waited. Finally they called and assured me that Willie was NOT there. They sat on the house for two days and never saw Willie, so they decided to "hit" the house. Willie's ex allowed them to search the premises. There was absolutely no indication that led them to believe he was there. No men's clothing, shoes, hats or anything that would point to a male living there. Upon searching the home thoroughly, they vacated and called me to tell me the bad news. I had to believe them on their word that they indeed did search for Willie, since I was hundreds of miles from the scene.

I know they "hit" the house because not long after they left, I received a call from Willie's ex and she blasted me up and down and two ways to Sunday because I had sent the dogs after him at her house. She was extremely upset at me, at them, AND at Willie. I did apologize and was able to diffuse her angst after a few minutes. By the time our conversation was over, I believed that Willie had never been there. If Willie was in the area, he wouldn't be for long because the heat was close by. I really thought he was there, so to get this info was a major disappointment. I couldn't relax because time was becoming another issue. All I kept thinking about was $65,000. I would drive by his trailer daily looking for any indication that he was, or might have been, there. I heard many different stories from his neighbors ranging from, "Yeah I saw him the other day" to "I haven't seen him in months." I would go to his trailer early in the morning and late at night. I was obsessed with finding this knucklehead. The results of my visits were a broken record. Everything remained the same. I even "set" the screen door like a booby trap to see if anyone entered or exited. Nothing, not one damn sign of Willie.

With a little more than two months remaining, I really needed to amp up the pressure on finding Willie. There was a running joke among my close friends because they had seen the WANTED picture I had printed in the local newspaper. Instead of "Hey, how are you?" it was "Hey, I saw Willie" or "I know where Willie is." Thank God my sense of humor eased my grinding teeth and white knuckles. Usually when money is offered publicly in return for a defendant's capture, it is just a matter of time before the criminal is located and apprehended. For some reason all the leads I got were dead ends.

One afternoon as I passed Willie's trailer home, I espied a "For Sale" sign outside his door. I slammed the brakes like I was landing an airbus at the teeny-tiny Meriden Markham Airport. I almost soiled my undies. Finally I had something to go on. If he had a real estate agent then at least ONE person could get in contact with him. I drove right over to the office of the real estate agent and explained my plight. I pleaded with him for information, but the real estate agent explained that he did not know where he was and that he had no way of getting in contact with him. He claimed he was hired by Willie, received a signed, legal permission document from Willie to list and sell the trailer, and that Willie would check in periodically regarding the status of any future sale. But he was adamant that Willie left no phone number and no address. What was I to do? I thought that maybe that was a line of dung I was getting, but I needed this agent to be an ally so I thanked him, gave him my card and asked him to pass a message along to Willie: I sure would like to have a word with him.

Even though the agent couldn't give me a phone number or new address, I saw a little glimmer of light in what had been a dark abyss. Willie had been close to home. Had Willie never left the area? Had he such a charismatic personality that not one soul would give him up? At least I had something to work with. After thinking about my next move for a few minutes, I decided to call one of my connections, a buddy who was a real estate agent. Luckily for me, he had a client who was looking to purchase a small home or trailer home. Wow, I knew of a trailer home that was for sale. I could not have had a better scenario fall in my lap. I convinced him to take a look at Willie's residence on behalf of his client. The day was set. I was staked out across the street from the trailer. The two real estate agents arrived simultaneously, much to my delight. I had hopes that Willie would be there. I had high hopes. Would Willie be there and open the door? Could the capture be imminent? Was this the day that I finally meet up with Willie?

Willie's agent opened the door with his own key, and all my hopes collapsed. It was obvious that Willie was nowhere to be found. When the seller's agent didn't even knock to see if the owner was home, that meant he KNEW that the owner was not home. Crap! The viewing only took about 5 minutes. Heck, what the hell is there to view in a 20x30 trailer or whatever the hell the measurements were? I was truly disappointed, but I was not going to give up. I knew I would get him. Positive mental attitude goes a long way in my opinion.

Both agents exited the trailer, climbed into their cars and proceeded out of the trailer park. I called my buddy via cellphone. He advised me that the place was totally empty. Nothing in it. No plates, no bed, no couch, no nothing. Not even a damn roll of toilet paper. His last remark to me was "Where's Willie?" My buddy and I like to bust each other's chops, so believe it or not, that remark made me laugh and it eased the painful thought of losing $65,000.

I basically was back to square one with Willie. No new leads, no one calling to say he had seen him, nothing. I was about sixty days away from writing out a big check for an inconsiderate dope pusher. The more I thought about it, the more I had to stop thinking about it because it gave me a nasty case of stomach rot. I call it gut rot. Just tore me up inside like I'd swallowed box cutter knives with the blades protruding. I couldn't let the loss of money lead me to the funny farm, so I just kept plugging away.

My luck and perseverance would soon pay off. While I was at the local courthouse doing my thing, a couple of days after the trailer home "showing," I was notified of yet another person who failed to appear and now I was on the clock like the NFL draft. I really didn't want to hear about another damn skip. I had my plate full, or should I say empty, with Willie. I called my office, got the telephone number for my latest skip and called it. The defendant's mom answered and told me the new address for the skip.

During lunch recess, I drove up to the new address. It was a pay by the day, week, or month quasi hotel/ motel with some efficiency units. I parked in front of the OFFICE sign and started to get out of my car. It was the middle of July and an especially comfortable, low humidity day. Not a cloud in the sky. As I stood up straight and looked towards the office door, I saw out of the outermost corner of my eye, about sixty feet away, a blond bombshell to my extreme right. I'm telling you her hair was so blond and radiant it could start a fire in an arid forest. She had on some pretty skimpy clothes with "stuff" hanging out all over. She had to be about 5'-9" or 5"-10", and she was strutting her stuff even though she was obviously upset.

As I focused my other eye on her, I noticed a short, medium-built guy, walking very quickly toward her, as if he was trying to stop her from leaving in a tizzy. I almost crapped my trousers. "That looks like Willie!!!" I screamed out internally. I watched them get into a late model car. The female was driving and the male rode shot gun. I couldn't believe it. I knew that it had to be Willie. It just had to be Willie.

As they approached my car, I ducked down a bit so they wouldn't see me and luckily my car shielded their view of me. I turned directly toward the oncoming car so I could get a good look at the passenger as it went by. Slowly the car passed me and I got a great look at the male passenger. It WAS Willie. I freaked out. I had been looking for this guy for 4 months and here he was. If I was dumb enough, I would have dove into his passenger window and probably broken my neck, but I just watched. For a split second our eyes met. I saw Willie and Willie saw me. After Willie saw me, his blond bombshell driver sped out of the parking lot like a NASCAR driver.

I knew that Willie had "made" me and now the chase was on. I got back in my car and pursued the dynamic duo. His lady friend was absolutely flooring it, weaving in and out of lanes trying to lose me. I called the local Police Department, described the car, its occupants and the direction they were heading. The cops knew there were active felony warrants for Willie because I reminded them just about every day. In fact, I would tell anyone that would listen to me that Willie was a wanted man. They radioed the chase to the nearby units. I drove as fast as possible without wrecking my car or getting into an accident, but I couldn't stay with Willie and his girl without endangering the public. The police and I scoured the area but Willie eluded detection and was again missing.

I eventually made it back to the hotel/motel and spoke with the manager. I felt like a monkey's uncle. Willie had taken up residence there for the past couple of weeks. I was shocked to hear that. I never thought he would be anywhere near the town where he was wanted. At this point, the manhunt for Willie was extensive. Unfortunately, I was the only real dog in the fight. No one would lose except me. Not the cops, not the hotel manager, not Willie's girl, just me. I was so close, yet so far from my absconder; it was maddening. The manager allowed me into his room and I searched for clues as to where he could be headed. I checked the closet, looked in his trash basket for receipts etc., and went through the drawers. I considered that, if he had the gumption to hang out in town, he might be real ballsy and return to the hotel for his meager belongings. The following forty eight hours, yeah just like the movie, were stressful. Once again I had a connection. One of my racquetball buddies lived adjacent to the hotel/motel in an end unit condo. That condo became my new home. I had a clear view of the room Willie was renting and I could see the window, the curtains, and any movement, while I sat there and waited. Many thoughts passed through my head when I was in this down time situation. I thought about how crazy my afternoon was. I had visions of Willie laughing at me as he sped by. I also thought about how MAD I would be if I didn't catch that little rascal. My guard was always up and the tension heightened with each minute that passed. My plan was to keep a close watch throughout the night looking for any signs of Willie or his girlfriend. Unfortunately, there was no movement, no curtains drawn, and no lights on or off, nothing.

I needed to think like a bail jumper to catch a bail jumper. Up until now, Willie had won the mental chess match, outwitting me for more than four months. I would later find out that he really didn't go too far. He just became like Ike and Tina's hit song, a "Rolling Stone." After brainstorming with some wily detectives at the cop shop, we figured that Willie wouldn't be too far. They sent a teletype to the surrounding towns describing Willie, and what car he could be in and the description of his girlfriend, now accomplice. After staying up all night and most of the next day on pure adrenaline, I finally crashed. I hadn't slept that soundly since my college days after a night out at the Village Pub on Whalley Ave. in New Haven, CT. Man, did they have the best Tabasco shooters and draft ale.

Then my phone rang. It was my police friend Les.

"Buck, we have your man" he exclaimed.

"Cut it out!" I snapped back at him in disbelief.

"You are kidding me right?"

"No, we HAVE Willie in custody" he assured me.

"Where?" I asked like a desperate beggar.

"Berlin PD. picked him up at a local motel, literally in bed with his girl," he replied.

"No shit?" I said doubtingly.

"Yes, he's here and he's in custody." He again stated.

What a great phone call to wake up to, and what a way to go out on a bang for Willie. If it had not been for the other person I initially went to look for at that address, Willie might still have been at large and my wallet would have been much lighter. By the way, the other bond skip promptly straightened out his case with the court and had the forfeiture vacated. Talk about luck! I got the two for one special that day. Case closed. Phhhweeww!!!

Somewhere Over Fishkill

Chapter Seven
Somewhere Over Fishkill

Benjamin H. was a decent person with an obvious drug problem. He grew up and lived all his life in the same town where he had run into some legal problems. As I mentioned, drugs and/ or alcohol are the common thread that is sewn into the fabric of most crimes. Benjamin became a victim of this very fabric. Here's the skinny on Benjamin: he was accused of committing several larcenies; he would binge on booze and drugs then go on a "shopping" spree in local neighborhoods, breaking into cars in the early morning and stealing anything of value. These crimes are called "smash and grabs." Benjamin needed money to support his habit. Living under the influence cost him his job, so he resorted to nefarious means to sustain himself.

My uncle, Weenik, the man that introduced me to this industry many moons ago, took on his bonds and wasn't surprised when Benjamin failed to appear. Weenik and I worked closely until he retired in 1995. I was usually by his side soaking up everything he could teach me to be successful in the industry. I would study his interaction with clients and co-signers alike and make mental notes on how to deal with all walks of life. To say the least, the foundation of excellent business practices he instilled in me was not built in sand. I would help in skip recovery and other aspects of the business. Weenik was always thinking ahead about his next move and that is one attribute that I still try to emulate.

We searched for Benjamin and discovered he had bolted the area and was gone. We asked around and just about everyone knew him, but hadn't seen him for some time. Some of the smash and grab victims were also looking for him, but for a different reason; they wanted their stuff back and they wanted to kick his derriere. After some intensive scouring of the local gins mills, we found out that Benjamin had fled to Lake Winola, Pennsylvania. Where the hell was Lake Winola, Pennsylvania? After a quick glance at an atlas, I discovered it was close to Scranton, PA. It just so happened, coincidentally, that Weenik had frequented that airport in his countless air trips. He was psyched up about flying back to Scranton and picking up Benjamin. We planned to go the next day but were delayed by the weather.

In a small four seat plane one has to take extra precautions weather-wise before embarking on a trip. Weenik had been stuck in various airports along the east coast due to weather factors, so he didn't want to take any chances. The next day the skies were clear but the wind that had ushered out the bad weather stayed. The flight plan was registered, the local cops were notified, and we were on our way to Lake Winola. Flying usually takes about one third the time of driving, so it made sense to fly, hopefully pick up Benjamin, and get back before the sun retired for the day. Up we went, heading west into a strong headwind that impeded our effort to get there quickly. Flying into the wind over mountains in a Cessna 182 is not the most stable ride one could have. The strong winds were knocking the plane up, down, and sideways without the courtesy of a warning gust. A few times my breakfast was having a game of tag with my uvula. The best medicine, I figured, was to look at Uncle Weenik. I can see it like it was yesterday. He always flew with his head cocked back about twenty degrees as if he was about to sneeze. He would wear a visored hat and a "flying" jacket. But Weenik never seemed concerned or worried about all the turbulence. He would just fly the damn plane without any emotion. Well, if he wasn't concerned, then why should I be concerned? Just seeing his demeanor helped me get over the fear of flying.

Don't get me wrong; Weenik liked to have some fun up in the air. He would do some mild acrobatic maneuvers with unsuspecting passengers. Just for the hell of it, he would cut the engine and we would do a free fall. Plummeting down without warning sometimes left my skivvies a bit messy, if you know what I mean. His other favorite stomach turner was increasing the airplane speed, jerking the steering wheel towards him, which meant a drastic ascension, and then slowly easing the wheel back. He would call them "loop de loops". I didn't know what to call them then, but now, I would call them "puke" de loops.

Weenik would never pull these stunts with a bail jumper in his plane; then he was all business.

We finally landed safely in Scranton, tethered the plane, paid the docking fee, and rented a car for our trip to apprehend Benjamin. Lake Winola was about a thirty minute ride northwest of the airport. Our only solid lead was that he was holed up in one of the lake cottages. That was it. Weenik and I arrived at the lake after a short, nondescript drive from the airport. We had the same thought; the lake was bigger than we expected. How the hell were we going to find this guy? There were countless cottages dotting the lake's edge. All we could do was drive around the lake and hope to spot Benjamin. We surmised that he had to have driven there somehow. As far as we knew, there was no other way to get there, no public busses or trains. So we slowly wove our way along the winding shoreline, peering down each dead end, rural roadway looking for Connecticut license plates. We went around the lake once, and found nothing.

We tried again and luckily for us, we hit pay dirt! As we inched our way toward some cottages without a waterfront beach access, we noticed a car with CT plates that wasn't there on our first orbit. It had to be him in that cottage. There was no way it couldn't be. Weenik and I deployed from our rental car and cautiously approached the cottage. In this part of Pennsylvania, I don't think much crime occurs, because the door was open and only a shabby screen door separated Weenik and me from the inside of that cottage. Without having actually seen Benjamin in the cottage, we could not legally enter the premises. We stole a look in through the screen and saw a living room that looked like a tornado had just come through it. I mean it was nasty looking and it smelled of rotting rot! Damn near chunked on the front stoop. After securing my nostrils from any further harassment using my thumb and index finger, I continued to assess the scene before me. We saw no movement, and heard no sign of a person, specifically Benjamin, within the confines of the cottage.

We walked around the back of the cottage that abutted some gnarly undergrowth, so mature that it had blocked the view of the pristine lake. The sight on the back deck of the cottage was no better. The deck was full of garbage piled high and wide, and I mean all sorts of garbage from food to beer bottles to clothes, and household trash. There must have been a dead animal or two thrown in as well. BUT, there was no sign of Benjamin. Where the hell was he? Weenik and I were at the only cottage on this freaking lake that had a car with Connecticut plates on its property. He had to be lurking around there somewhere.

All of a sudden we heard some noise originating from underneath the deck of the house next door. If not for THAT noise we wouldn't have heard any noise. It was so quiet that even an insomniac could have fallen asleep.

Weenik and I cautiously crept down the slope and faced the back of the house listening very carefully. Under the deck was a small door no bigger than four feet high, and three-four feet wide, and it was slightly open. Then, we heard some more commotion from behind the door made for the likes of the lollipop kids. Well, we didn't travel this far NOT to check out the noise. Could it be a wild animal? Could it be our imagination? Was the sinister wind playing tricks on our minds? Was Benjamin behind that door? Was I on "Let's Make a Deal" with Monty Hall? Our only option was to check out what was behind that little door.

We slowly opened the door. Luckily the sunlight was able to expose about three feet into the crawlspace/ storage space. BAM!

"Benjamin"! I yelled. "Benjamin, come the hell out of there."

I could see Benjamin plain as day now that the little door was opened fully and its front was now kissing the foundation of the house. Benjamin decided to dismiss my request by paying me no mind.

"Benjamin, get the hell out of there!!" I yelled more sternly.

Benjamin looked at me, then right through me. He had the dead eyes of a great white shark. As I crouched down to enter the dank crawlspace, Benjamin asked who we were. We told him, but it just didn't register. Then we smelled the most distinguishable odor. It was turpentine, a smell that is unique and unforgettable. The crawlspace reeked of turpentine. I covered my nose with the bottom of my shirt and entered. My eyes started watering, and I was in no mood to negotiate with Benjamin. I yanked him out and he sprawled out on to the weedy lawn behind the cottage. Weenik and I easily cuffed him as I kept him steady and brought him to his feet. Benjamin could hardly stand still, or stand period.

He had been under the house in his private sanctuary sniffing freakin' paint thinner. What the hell? Even out in the open air he reeked like a paint thinner warehouse. If someone lit a cigarette, Benjamin would have been a victim of spontaneous combustion. Benjamin still had no idea what was going on. He didn't recognize us. I guess turpentine did a number on his thinker. I've heard some crazy things, but paint thinner? Damn, that's desperation and an evil addiction. We convinced Benjamin that we were not Lucifer's henchmen, or angels for that matter, and we were going back to Connecticut so he could face his accusers. He still didn't fully understand what was happening, but he agreed to go with us. At least we gave him an option: YOU agree to GO with us now or WE TAKE you with us now. Benjamin settled on GO. We drove back to the airport with the windows down to thin out the turpentine stench.

Before long we were up in the air with that strong wind now at our backs. I sat in the back seat with Benjamin while Weenik piloted the plane eastward. Benjamin was still muddled but seemed to be gaining his senses. He was becoming more alert and attentive as we flew. I unfortunately noticed that he had a vicious case of nasal oyster drip losing its battle with gravity. Finally about three quarters of the way home, somewhere over Fishkill, NY, I think, Benjamin snapped out of his drug delirium and realized his impending fate. He recognized Weenik and me and asked how he got into the plane and where we were taking him. He had no recollection of what had transpired the last couple of hours. He was not buying the hiding in the crawlspace sniffin' turpentine story we were layin' on him. He thought he was dreaming the whole time. I guess Benjamin's brand of turpentine really disoriented his cognitive perception. As quickly as Benjamin had taken flight with drugs and airplanes, his free ticket back to jail was about to be punched like a conductor on a train. Neeeext stop-City jail. The moral of the story: only painters should use paint thinner!

The Intersection That Time Forgot

Chapter Eight
The Intersection That Time Forgot

Samantha I. liked to live life on someone else's dime; she was a good time Charlie type. She grew up and spent most of her life east of the Connecticut River in an enclave of a lakeside town. Samantha had a penchant for getting close to endearing, unsuspecting men, and draining them of their savings. She had taken up residence with Gerald, a lonely, elderly man who supported her. Gerald owned his home with no outstanding mortgage and had a decent monthly pension. I suppose they were good for each other in many ways, until Samantha decided to pilfer his antique gun collection for drug money. Samantha was picked up on a gun theft charge and incarcerated. After bail was set at arraignment, I was contacted by Samantha's house mate asking me to post the $5,000 bond on Samantha's behalf. Even though Gerald knew she was the person accused of stealing his gun collection, he insisted on posting bail for her. These kinds of cases usually end favorably for the defendant. If there is not a cooperating witness then the burden of proof becomes a problem for the State's Attorney. After assessing the situation, I decided to underwrite the bail bond for Samantha.

It wasn't long before Gerald finally realized he made a big mistake. Not only did Samantha take off, leaving him with a $5,000 liability, she cleaned him out of all his valuables while he was away from the house one afternoon. He immediately contacted me to tell me what happened and I advised him to file another police report. Samantha may have burned him, but she had not missed court yet, so there was not much I could do. Her original gun theft case was set down for a motion, about a month after her latest act of thievery. Hopefully she would surface and all would be well. I figured she would come back with some sob story and he would take her back in. If that didn't happen, her drug addiction would probably win the battle of wills and she would commit another crime to survive. Thus, if she was arrested on a new offense, with an active FTA warrant on the books, that would exonerate me from paying the forfeiture; she would be served with the failure to appear warrant and detained.

On the date of her next appearance in court, there was no sight of Samantha. Gerald was there, and I was there, but Samantha was missing in action. The bail was ordered forfeited with the statutory six month stay of that forfeiture imposition. Gerald asked me what "bond forfeiture" meant and I wasted no time in telling him he was now responsible to me for the $5,000. He wasn't too pleased, to say the least, and vowed to find her, come hell or high water. As we parted, I told him to call me if he found anything out about Samantha. I was concerned about the forfeiture, but I knew that the co-signer would be able to cough up the dough if necessary. He assured me that I would not lose a penny on this case. Most co-signers that are on the hook for a bail bond usually make idle threats directed at the absconders, and I just pass it off as chatter. This guy was serious. His words were violent and his body language was that of an angry pit bull. He was ripping mad because he had been wangled by this squirrely broad. The sugar ran out on the Sugar Daddy!!

Over the next several weeks, I periodically telephoned Gerald. He sounded depressed and swore he was shaking every bush and turning every stone to find his bitter/sweetness, Samantha. My efforts were minimal because I didn't have much to work with, and I knew he would pay in the end, so I put the case on the bottom of my forfeiture pile. Speaking of my forfeiture pile, this is a pile that never ever goes away. The pile seems to take on a life of its own. It fluctuates like a patient with a bad heart who's having an EKG test. I may have a stack of 15-20 bonds skips, and then within a week it's down to five or six. Sometimes the criminals commit new crimes and get served with the FTA, or they are involved in a traffic stop, identified and taken into custody. Some realize running is no way of life and turn themselves in. If I am able to make contact with them, I first attempt to reason calmly with them and explain their options. I must admit, some bond jumpers don't go anywhere; they just ignore their court appearance requirement. A simple phone call to them usually prompts them to rectify the forfeiture. Do they really want to run and hide and live a sheltered life for the REST of their life? Do they think they're going to outsmart everyone? Do they want to screw over their co-signers? Most skippers come to their senses after reasoning out their options and or alternatives. Some just don't get it.

Some absconders have no faith in the criminal justice system, and therefore treat it with contempt. Over the years I've seen defendants, who, in their opinion, have been shafted by the system. The thought of bias leads them to be uncooperative with the court procedure. Unfortunately, there are some glaring inconsistencies from one courthouse to the next, partly because of the sheer volume of business at any given courthouse. Each judge has an opinion and it may not be the same as another judge in another court. Although they may both be correct, their ultimate imposition of a sentence may be quite different.

Who knows what Samantha was thinking? Maybe Samantha had hoped for a lenient judge. Was she going to be sent to the slammer?

Would the judge show any mercy? How could she face Gerald after she scammed him? Only she could answer these questions.

Unexpectedly, I received a phone call from Gerald.

"Biesteks" I answered, as I usually do.

"Is this Mr. Biestek?" The caller asked excitedly.

"Yes it is, may I ask who is calling?" I replied.

"It's Gerald, you know Sama…. ".

Before he could finish spitting out her name I asked what news he had for me.

Gerald declared, "She's in Texas!"

Sugar Daddy Gerald went on to tell me that Samantha had written him a letter and had given him her new address. Once again, she was trying to work her charm. I asked Gerald to read me the postmark on the outside of the envelope. He said it was from Texas, Hillsboro, TX. She didn't leave a phone number but explained via the letter she was tired of running and was desperate. She said she was living in the middle of nowhere and was shacked up with some convict from Arizona.

Samantha had run out of options, and had the gall to try her luck with Gerald one more time. She didn't say she wanted to come home; she wrote Gerald asking for money! Can you believe the stones on this chick? In this industry one can never say one has seen it all because there is always another angle that the suspected criminal will think about. The BS stories and explanations are never ending. Gerald wanted this girl bad, but not in a "bad way." Being a sugar daddy comes with some perks and favors, but that part of his relationship with Samantha had been terminated.

Suffice it to say, he was willing to do anything to see her behind bars. I advised Gerald to respond with kind words and trick her into believing he would help her. After several letters back and forth to each other, he made it seem as though she had gained his trust. He said he needed to cash in some CDs before he could send her money. He also told her it would take a few days, so he asked her to be patient.

Gerald and I discussed his options. Do nothing and eat the $5,000. OR send me and my bounty help to Texas to get her. He wanted her back in jail, so I was on a flight to Dallas - Fort Worth (DFW) within a couple of days.

My help, remember Natalie, would join me in Dallas the day after I arrived. Our plan was for me to go down to Dallas early, find an inexpensive hotel, rent a car, then drive that oil-rig-ridden, cow country drive down highway 67, through Waxahachie and into Hillsboro, to case out the address provided by the defendant herself. Hopefully I'd confirm that she was residing there and then go back to Dallas and pick up Natalie who would be arriving on a late night flight.

My flight from LaGuardia International Airport (LGA) was a very early flight; I think 6:00 A.M., so I was up and at 'em about 2:30 A.M. I took a quick rinse shower to wake up and I was in my car driving down to New York in no time. The three hour flight seemed to pass by quickly because my mind was focused on formulating a plan of attack to bring back Samantha. After arriving at DFW, I quickly rented a car and was headed towards Arlington on I-20. Being a huge baseball fan, I chose a modest hotel close to the Rangers' Ballpark at

Arlington. I was psyched because the Rangers were in town that night and I would be able to see them play my favorite team, the L.A. Angels, and root against the home team. Also, the hotel wasn't too far from the airport, which was convenient for picking up Natalie later that evening.

After checking in and unpacking my one carry on piece of luggage, I grabbed a quick bite to eat and headed towards Hillsboro in search of Samantha. This was my first recon mission in Texas, so I relished the views of open space and oil rigs pounding away, making some lucky bastards billionaires. The directions I had took me off the main road onto a farmer's road of sorts. I say farmer's road, because once I was on this tract of roadway, I felt like a farmer. I was driving along a slinking, skinny road surrounded by corn stalks. Dust and dirt flew from the tires of my rental car and the May, Texas sun was beasting itself upon my windshield as thousands upon thousands of errant particles filled the atmosphere. I was thinking I must be lost because I hadn't seen any sign of life other than the crops. Upon coming over a knoll, not the infamous grassy knoll, I saw an intersection with a structure on each corner. On my right at the intersection was a church. On my left was an old store converted into a residence. Diagonally across from the old store was another church, and the final structure was an old, dilapidated, simple, square-shaped one story home next to the converted store. The scene could have been in a "Twilight Zone" episode. I had reached the intersection that time forgot. I bet that one hundred years prior to my driving up to the intersection, everything looked exactly the same, except for some weathering on the structures.

I was at the address that Samantha provided to Gerald, and I was very doubtful that she would be found at this location. There were no signs of life but for a dog chained up outside of the converted store. It was some sort of Labrador and it was just keeping cool in the shade. Upon further inspection, I noticed the door to the converted store had a padlock on the outside. I thought that was strange. I know the dog didn't have the key, so maybe I was going to have some Texas success. I double checked the address against the dust covered street marker. This was the place. Now that I knew how long it took to get there, and knew where it was, I quickly bolted back to Dallas. I was extremely tired from the stress of traveling, and being in an unfamiliar place. The Texas sun felt like August New England sun and totally wiped me out. I knew I had to get back so I could go take in the Rangers game, cheering on my beloved Angels, and I floored it back to the hotel and rested for a bit. I set the alarm clock for 6:30 P.M., just in case I nodded off, which I did. Rudely awakened from a sound slumber, I cleaned up and headed to the ballpark. What a beautiful place to see a game. The cool evening air descended upon north central Texas and it felt soothing. I couldn't tell you who won the game, but it was a nice break from the tension I had experienced earlier and the stress I would soon experience the following day when I would try to apprehend Samantha. When Natalie's flight arrived around 11:30 P.M., I picked her up and we went to the hotel. As I checked her into her room, I said, "Get some rest…we are out of here at 0600."

Morning came way too soon, and I was still exhausted. I went down the hall, knocked on Natalie's door and when she opened it, she was packed and ready to go. What a true professional. We checked out of our rooms and were off to Hillsboro. During our ride, I explained to her what the layout was like and described the intersection. As the powerful sun stabbed the landscape with its sharp beams of light, I had a serious case of déjà vu. Wasn't I just on this road? Natalie and I safely arrived in Hillsboro, and we went to the sheriff's office to let him know our intentions with Samantha. The sheriff was a tough looking, no nonsense, you-better-look-me-in-the-eye son, macho type police guy. He didn't want to hear any of what we were telling him. I couldn't have been any more professional or courteous in speaking with him. As I said, he didn't want to hear anything. In fact he said, and I quote:

"If I hayiv to cahm out thar be cawszz of yawl cawwszin inny praaaahhhblems in mah county thayin aahm takin ya both ee-in."

Yeah, try to figure that mess out. I almost needed an interpreter, so just phonetically sound it out slowly and some form of the English language will take shape.

"Yes sir", was all I could say.

Natalie and I got the hell out of his office. We would have beaten Superman if he raced us out of Mr. Charming's command post. We proceeded to the rental car mumbling under our breath and off we went down that dirt road to the intersection that time forgot. What I thought of the sheriff's hospitality is not printable material.

We finally reached our destination, and Natalie had the same reaction I had a day earlier. She, too, thought she was in a time warp. It was do or die, so we exited the car and first went to the shabby square home next to the converted store. We knocked. No reply. Again we knocked, and received no reply. That Labrador next door decided to start barking like he had been bitten by a wasp. I mean that boy was yappin' away. If anyone was home in either house, someone would be coming outside, probably with a twelve gauge blaster, not to mention an itchy and elated trigger finger. The laws are a bit different in Texas. We were targets even if we were doing nothing wrong. "Don't mess with Texas" resonated loudly in my head, and replaying the words of that prick sheriff didn't help matters.

We checked the converted store and saw no movement. This was not good--no Samantha and no luck. We didn't have a lot of time to hang around. I thought it would be easy. Ya know, we'd knock on the door, she'd open it, she'd put her hands behind her back, say, "Take me back," and then we'd be gone. As we thought about our next move and what course of action we would take, the dog calmed down and stopped yapping. Maybe it did get stung, or maybe the dog saw us as no threat. Natalie noticed women's clothing sticking out of a trash can behind the house. She opened the lid and discovered letters that Gerald had written to Samantha, tossed in the garbage. We WERE at the right house after all. But Samantha had either moved or just plain old wasn't home. We decided to check with the closest neighbors.

In the far distance we detected a farm house with a towering silo rising above the acres upon acres of corn stalks. This farmhouse was in the opposite direction from the highway. We decided to go and see if whoever lived there knew Samantha. It took us a couple of minutes to drive there. We exited the car and approached the front door, which was open, protected only by a flimsy screen.

"Hello, HELLO, hello, any one home?"

I questioned the inside of the ranch house. No one replied.

I repeated, "Hello," in a much louder voice. No one home, no one working in the fields, what the hell was going on? Natalie and I were starting to realize this was a potential bust-out, wasted mission. As we walked back to the car in the driveway and anticipated a "losers" ride back to the airport, we heard a dog barking in the direction of that now famous intersection. Yes, THAT dog. Sound traveled a long way because there were few trees to intercept it. We both knew that the dog was the dead giveaway. The dog had to be barking because someone was home. Samantha?? We got back in the car, and floored it back to the intersection like Boss Hogg and Daisy Dukes. Even Robert De Niro in Midnight Run would have been proud of us.

We got to the house and noticed the dog was not outside chained up, well, like a dog, and that the padlock was off the door, which was ajar, allowing access to the converted store.

Someone was in that house, and we had no time to hesitate. We softly knocked on the door and we were invited in, much to our surprise. Quickly, we entered through the open door in to the house, where we both saw Samantha. She turned to us and instantly realized that she was bagged. She knew my face and she became distraught. Within a matter of moments we took her into custody. We finally had Samantha within our domain and needed to quickly high tail it out of that county. I didn't need any headaches from the sheriff, and we didn't have time to waste getting to our scheduled flight. We quickly got in the car and raced towards the airport. If traffic was not a problem, we would make it to DFW with about an hour to spare. Samantha was relatively calm on the ride back and several times pleaded with us to let her go. We were not hearing any of that. Just like the sheriff. Don't think for one minute that I forgot about the sheriff. His words still echo in my head. I was driving as fast as I could, LEGALLY, out of HIS County. I didn't need any unwanted stops on our way back.

We arrived at the airport without any delay and proceeded to give Samantha the old "You'd better behave yourself" lecture. To stay under the radar, we uncuffed Samantha and told her to act like a lady through security. We told her if authorities found out who she was, they would take her into custody for the gun charges in Connecticut, and they would have to extradite her back. All this was true and Samantha realized she was better off with us now, than wallowing in a Texas prison for who knows how long.

Once in the air, Natalie and I were able to let down our guard a bit. Where could Samantha run to now?? Thirty three thousand feet is a hell of a jump. We had over three hours to relax and feel good about our accomplishment.

The rest of the recovery mission went smoothly and Samantha was deposited into the local jail. I called Gerald and he was ecstatic that his little princess was finally back home in a jail cell.

We knew that Samantha had been living with an ex-con, but I wasn't aware, until about a week later, that Samantha had been living with a paroled MURDERER from Arizona. Lucky for us, he wasn't home when we came for Samantha. REAL lucky.

Cornbread and Fixins

Chapter Nine
Cornbread and Fixins

Leonard S. was a tall, skinny, eighteen year old kid living with his aunt in central Connecticut. He wasn't the sharpest tool in the shed, but his polite and respectful personality made up for his inability to join the Mensa club. He was staying with his aunt because his mama had moved back down South and Leonard wanted to stay up North with his friends. He also wanted to finish high school, so I give him credit for that. Living with Auntie wasn't like living with Mama. Mama wouldn't put up with a lot of misbehavior. Auntie, by nature of the relationship, was a little more lenient. Auntie's leniency, in respect to Leonard, was to a fault, and as a result, Leonard started to really screw up in school and out on the streets. He was hanging with the wrong crowd, and was easily persuaded into criminal acts due to his lack of good judgment. Ultimately, Leonard became a patsy for his boys, and it wasn't long before he found himself facing a felony assault charge. He allegedly beat up one of his girlfriends so badly that she was hospitalized. After arraignment, he called his auntie from the county jail and pleaded with her to get him the hell outta there. This was Leonard's first time in county and he wasn't digging it. All the BS talk on the street he had grown accustomed to didn't help him in the slammer. Leonard was desperate to get out and he was definitely scared. Auntie had grown tired of Leonard's antics, but because he was family, she reluctantly posted his $25,000 bond. As with every co-signer, I gave her the spiel regarding FTA and the forfeiture process, yada yada yada, and she agreed.

Leonard's court proceedings didn't go as well as expected. He was in one of those smaller courts, so they took a real close look at his case and were not going to budge; they wanted Leonard to do some time. The only other option was a trial and if Leonard lost, chances were very good that he'd be sent up the river for an extended "time out." Heck, to me, one hour would be a long time; Leonard was facing a few years. Everyone has the right to a (fair) trial, but if he loses, the punishment generally is much more significant than the original plea offer. Usually the first offer by the State's Attorney is the most punishment that would be acceptable to the people of the state, then as time goes on and witnesses change stories or are unwilling to testify, the state usually "comes off the charge" and offers less of a punishment. Leonard's case dragged on for a few months. It was my understanding that the victim/witness against Leonard could not be located. Without the cooperation of the victim, the state would probably not have had much of a case.

Leonard didn't stick around to find out. He eventually failed to appear and was among the missing. Now, Leonard faced an additional five years jail time, just for missing court on a felony assault charge. What a knucklehead, trading 5-10 years of his life in prison, for a few weeks, days, or months living the "look over your shoulder" life. I immediately called Auntie and gave her the bad news. Auntie knew Leonard had booked because she hadn't seen him for a few days leading up to his court date. Auntie was a nice, polite lady, who had a good job with the Board of Education, and the poor woman damn near fainted when I told her she was on the hook for the $25,000. To save her own behind, she immediately got on the phone and called Anthony's mama in Alabama. Mama said Leonard had been there recently, with some new girlfriend from up North. She also explained that Leonard wasn't living with her, but was somewhere in the area.

That's all I needed to hear. Within a few days I was on my way to Frisco City, Alabama with a rookie bounty hunter. The rookie was my ever-loving, beautiful wife, Nurse. Remember, my entire family has nicknames. Come to think of it I tend to give a lot of people a certain moniker. Some of them I say it to their face and others I use if I am referring to them in conversation. It's just something I've done my whole life. Anyway, Nurse was duly appointed an official Buck B. bounty hunter. This was her big debut out in my chosen profession. The timing for her joining me on this expedition was perfect. Neither one of us had ever been to Alabama, so we would kind of make it a little get away for us. As any parent knows, especially a parent of 3 children, getaways are quite refreshing. This trip would be all business until Leonard was in custody OR Leonard was not able to be located. If I bagged Leonard, I would deposit him into a local jail and the state of Connecticut would extradite him back to Connecticut. Whether we got him or not, our final destination would be Gulf Shores, AL.

Nurse and I flew into Mobile in a torrential down pour. She is not a big fan of take offs and landings and this landing over the bay was bumpy beyond imagination. The small plane bounced, bobbed, and wove, as though it were in the ring with Muhammad Ali. Even I had sweaty palms. I imagined the headlines back home; LOCAL COUPLE PERISH IN ALABAMA AIR DISASTER. It was good to be at the gate deplaning after that stressful landing. Our guardian angels must have called in a favor for us on that day; as soon as we got into our Ford convertible Mustang rental (Nurse loves Ford Mustangs), the skies parted like a Bible story and the Alabama sun shone brightly. What a country, huh?

We made our way onto interstate highway 65, which basically bisects the state. Continuing northeasterly, we crossed over a couple of rivers and then turned off and headed north on highway 59. My irises had never seen such scenery along the way. We rolled along open fields, meadows, and plenty of cotton fields. I was enthralled by the cotton fields, which looked like snow. I was used to seeing snow, but never cotton fields. The endless acres of puffy cotton balls were a treat for both of us to see. We drove through itty bitty towns like Tensaw, Blacksher, Uriah, and Megargel before we arrived in Frisco City, a town of about fifteen hundred folks. There wasn't much to the town, and judging by the appearance of the dilapidated marquee advertising outdated movies, the town looked about five years behind the rest of the world. Life there seemed to be slow and easy.

Our first stop was to the local police department for a brief meeting and to introduce myself. The police station was very small and looked like a mobile trailer. I asked Nurse to stay in the car while I went in the front door of the building to let the troops know my intentions. Not knowing what to expect, I was pleasantly surprised at my reception. The secretary and the lone detective were the nicest people you would ever want to meet; they were more than helpful with answering all of my questions and they treated me with utmost professionalism and respect. The sheriff down in Hillsboro, Texas could have learned a lesson or two on how to welcome visitors from these fine people. In fact, I've traveled throughout the entire Southeast, and the people that reside in that section of our great country are the most hospitable I've met. I have found in my travels that my fellow northeasterners seem to be stuck in the Puritan ages, and tend to be a bit unfriendly and aloof.

I had a fact-filled conversation with the detective who actually knew Leonard and every other denizen of his small town. He said he had seen Leonard recently at his mama's house. The detective was unaware at the time that Leonard was wanted for felony assault in Connecticut. As I said earlier, Leonard was a respectful and polite kid. Now I know where he picked up those good qualities. I was sure they were instilled in him by the fine southern people here in Frisco City. The officer gave me his cell phone number and directions to Leonard's mama's house. He said, "Yawl cawl mi if yawl faaahhnd Lenahd, heeya?"

I'm not sure if a question mark is appropriate after "heeya" or if that should be a period after "heeya." I couldn't thank him enough and departed, having been graced with the best that humanity has to offer.

Leonard's mama's house was about three minutes away. Frisco City isn't that big, so navigating around was quite simple, even for this dumb Polack. Nurse and I pulled up to the suspect's home, just past a set of railroad tracks. We were eyeballed by a host of people idling around the driveway. The family must have been thinking, what the hell is going on here? I surmised that our convertible Mustang was the problem, not us. Around these parts, most cars are pick-ups or older cars, so pulling up in this car was like a UFO landing at Roswell, NM. We got out of the car with a "hat in hand" approach, and asked if Leonard was home. There had to be 10 people standing around the property and not one of them flinched or even acknowledged our existence. As I politely repeated my inquiry, I scanned the people hanging around as if I were a periscope rotating from a submarine in a deliberate and slow manner. I was hoping to ID Leonard. I must have seen a mirage because three or four of the idlers looked like Leonard. As I walked closer to the crowd of people, I was finally greeted with a "Can ah help yawl?" from one of the older gentlemen.

I again asked if Leonard was home. The gentleman asked who I was and I went into the whole thing again, like I did with the detective at the PD. Finally he yelled out, "Mama, come outside." Mama must have been inside cooking because the emanation coming from the house was mouthwatering. Eventually, Mama came out and asked if she could help me. After my third recital of my little spiel, Mama declared that Leonard was not there and wouldn't be coming back there. Just about an hour earlier, she explained to me, two nasty bounty hunters from Florida had come looking for Leonard.

They claimed he jumped bond in Pensacola and they were there to take him back. Can you believe it? What are the odds of four bounty hunters from two different states looking for the same person within an hour of each other?

Mama told me, as she told the other bounty hunting crew that Leonard had been there, but flew the coop because things were getting too hot for him to stay. He respected his mama too much to get her involved with his complicated criminal conundrum. The Florida bounty hunters missed Leonard by about an hour and we missed Leonard by about two hours. I just couldn't believe it. I've been fibbed to before, but I can tell you, Mama was not lying. She was one of God's angels. Mama even invited us to stay for lunch. She said the cornbread and fixins were just about done and the ribs and sides were ready. We almost took her up on her offer, but graciously declined. We exchanged phone numbers and promised to keep in touch if either one of us heard anything pertaining to Leonard. Now we understood the reason for the "cold shoulder" when we first arrived. They likened us to the Florida thugs, but then realized that we were not of the same ilk. Proof positive of this deduction was the lunch invitation offered by Mama. Obviously, our chance of finding Leonard at his mama's house, in Frisco City was a big fat zero, so Nurse and I headed to our final destination in Alabama, Gulf Shores.

On our way down to the Gulf, we took a different way back to see more of Alabama. We headed west on highway 84, then south on highway 65, then south on highway 59 through Bay Minette, and Foley before arriving in Gulf Shores. What with the travel, the drive north through the cotton fields, the police department, our initial cold reception, Mama's kindness, and the drive back down to the Gulf, we had had a pretty full day.

The sights and sounds of the emerald Gulf of Mexico made the entire journey worthwhile. It was time to relax and forget about work. We checked into a spectacular, high rise condo planted right on the Gulf. The views overlooking the sparkling whitecaps on the horizon of the Gulf were of brochure vintage. We spent the next few days exploring the region from Fort Morgan to the west, spanning over to Orange Beach and Pensacola, Florida to our east. The weather was beautiful, as expected, and the time spent together without kids was much needed. I called Mama a couple of times and we chatted for a bit. It was like she was my own mama. I can't tell you enough about how nice this lady was. In fact, long after this case was over (every case eventually closes), I still kept in contact with her. I was fascinated by her charm and southern accent, and she enjoyed my friendship and strange accent as well.

Nurse and I flew back to Connecticut, without holding on for dear life this time, and unfortunately, without Leonard. I have to admit I wasn't that upset. Sometimes you have to just take it for what it's worth. It was a bust and I would probably have to eat the bond unless a miracle was going to happen.

I set up a meeting with the State's Attorney to fill him in on my travels to Alabama in hopes of bringing back Leonard. Sometimes, pleading my case helps me with final results. The State's Attorney decided to consult with Leonard's victim and get her feelings on the case. His investigator tried every method to locate the victim, and had no success. My second and final meeting with the State's Attorney regarding Leonard's case turned out better than I expected. I explained that Leonard would probably never enter Connecticut willingly, that Florida wanted him for some criminal activity, and I spent time and money flying to and from Alabama. I tried to apprehend the defendant and had proof to show for it. After considering all the factors, the State's Attorney decided to re-docket the matter and nolled the case. This meant that Buck B. was off the hook for the twenty five big ones, and that was well worth my efforts. I saw another part of the country, met the nicest people on this planet, made a friend in Mama, spent some quality time with my beautiful wife, and saved myself from writing out a big fat check. Boy do I love this job-- at times.

Doomsday Arrives

Chapter Ten
Dooms Day Arrives

Newton C. was quite the con man, good at the art of exploitation for his own benefit, and great at bilking people out of money, including moi. He was by no means a violent man; in fact, he was very personable, but almost every venture he was involved with had a shady side to it. I don't think he had done an honest day's work his entire life. He truly was a wolf in sheep's clothing.

Newton didn't like to earn money legally. He was skilled at conniving and had an advanced degree in larceny. By mere appearance, one would never suspect his unsavory talents, but deep down he would have to be one of the top ten most evil people I've come across in this industry. He didn't have an addiction problem, had a longtime girlfriend, and was a fairly responsible parent, so why do I call him an evil person? Well, because he stuck me for a large sum of cash, to put it simply. Newton put on the good guy act, but that was a disguise. He didn't give a shit about anyone or anything but himself. In other words, he could shake your right hand with his and steal your wallet with his left hand simultaneously. He embraced this way of life and was darn proud of it. What a fu%&in' phony!!

I had posted bond for him and his family on several occasions, and not once did a problem arise. Newton would always make his appearances. I was called upon to post a large bond ($75,000) on his behalf and I did so without hesitation because I had known Newton and his family for many years. He was a con artist weasel, but a con artist weasel that I could trust, or so I thought. Newton had run afoul of the law once again by getting pinched for possession of narcotics with intent to sell. I thought he would be a safe bet and that my bond would not be forfeited because Newton would never jump bond on me. As a matter of opinion, no one person is truly evil until he jumps bond on me, or he is my devious, devilish, competitor.

Prior to going to trial, the State's Attorney offered him a short jail sentence with probation to follow. Newton was getting up in age for a scamming criminal, so he and his pompous attitude declined the state's offer and took no plea bargain. He hired one of the best attorneys in the state and figured he would beat the rap. The prospective new home which he would have checked into immediately wasn't his idea of a vacation. The case was eventually put on the trial list and he would have to be available on short notice to begin with the proceedings.

Newton's case would be called in occasionally for resolution, but Newton's attorney and the state couldn't reach an amicable agreement for disposition. Calling in cases on the jury list to try to work out a deal is a common practice. The case seemed to drag on for months and Newton attended faithfully with his hot shot lawyer by his side.

Finally, Newton had his day and court and the trial commenced. Both sides argued their points, and after a couple of days, the case went to the jury for deliberation. A guilty verdict came back within hours. The judge sentenced Newton to more jail time than was originally offered during pre-trial discussions, (the amount of time escapes me but I think it was about three years). Luckily for Newton, the judge granted an appeal bond enabling him to remain free during the appeal process if he chose to, and could afford to, post the appeal bond. At that time of his sentencing, I was officially released from the liability of the original $75,000 bond.

Newton's family once again called upon me to post his appeal bond, which was set at $125,000. With no prior problems with him appearing, and the fact that he showed up for a trial and his sentencing date, I accepted the risk.

After a two plus year appeal review process, the three panel judges' verdict finally came down. The conviction was upheld and Newton was required to report to the court to begin his sentence. You guessed it. That despicable, diarrhea- diaper drenched, dastardly degenerate failed to appear. Doomsday arrived. His attorney called me and advised me that the judge had ordered the $125,000 bond forfeited. He further advised me to try and get Newton in court before the end of the court session and MAYBE, just maybe things would be okay.

I should have known that though he was a soft spoken, polite fellow, it was just a front. He was a snake in the grass waiting to strike on any unsuspecting victim, and I became another one of his victims.

I promptly called Newton's home number and spoke to his longtime girlfriend. She said he gave her a kiss goodbye, and said he was on his way to court to begin his jail sentence. I had a hard time believing that line of BULL. She was always there by his side every other court appearance and that day, a day that couldn't be topped by any other, she let him go to court alone. Something was rotten in Denmark. I pleaded with her to get a hold of him and have him call me pronto.

This was an obvious set up by the both of them. She was a co-conspirator in regards to him fleeing the area. As the day turned into evening, my stomach turned to knots. This was by far the largest potential monetary loss, forfeiture-wise, that I had to deal with in my life. What made it worse, I found out that the "house "Newton and his girl had resided in the last 10 years was a rental. They didn't even own it. I felt like such a schlub! Wait one second and let me get the bag of Morton's salt because the wound just kept growing. On top of all that disappointing news, I discovered the girlfriend wasn't employed. It appeared I had nothing or no one to go after except for the thief who ran away with my $125,000 bond. I know you're thinking that I'm a dummy for taking on such a risk without any collateral, but it is the nature of the business. Newton and his girlfriend had befriended me, and then took me to the cleaners! Now the joke was on me. I'm not dealing with angels, don't forget. So one day I love this job and the next day I'm feeling like an abused dog on my seventh and final day at an animal shelter. Can you say euthanize?

The chase was on and I couldn't wait to hunt Newton down, because this situation was now a personal vendetta. I talked to EVERYONE I knew who had been associated with Newton. I went back to the bar where he was arrested and displayed his picture everywhere. I went to his rental and sat on it for hours, hoping to catch that furtive fink coming or going. I constantly called his girl and explained that SHE would be responsible for the $125,000 because HE blew off court. As I look back in hindsight, SHE really didn't seem to give a rat's ass about MY problem.

There is a fine line that I have to walk with the co-signers. They must be treated as allies. If I were to blast her verbally, she would not be very cooperative. She wasn't very cooperative anyway, but I had to keep the door of communication open. She was my only lifeline to Newton. She knew where he was and I needed to get it out of her right quick!

As weeks passed by, I still didn't have a solid line on Newton or his whereabouts. This was bugging my NART (natural and reasonable tendencies) immensely. Newton was a seasoned criminal and probably spent the time during his appeal process setting up a new identity, so he could flee if the appeal wasn't in his favor. Everyone I spoke to either didn't know where he was or just didn't want to give him up. Usually money talks and BS walks and I had a substantial cash reward out on the streets for Newton. Even after the reward was posted, I still had nothing to work with.

Then the call came in from you know who. Newton apologized for putting me in this predicament and promised to pay me the entire bond forfeiture soon. Yeah, and the moon is made of cheese. Newton explained he had a friend who was going to shell out his bail money relatively soon. As far as I was concerned, I wanted either Newton, or the money. I didn't give a shit which one, but it had to be soon. If Newton turned himself in, or was captured by law enforcement, I'd be off the hook. If Newton or a benefactor reimbursed me for my losses, then I'd be good with that as well. I just didn't want to lose money because he decided to blow off court. I should mention that often people would rather pay large amounts of cash to me, instead of just taking care of the case. I always advise them that appearing is the way to go. However, even if I am reimbursed for my losses, that doesn't make the warrant for failure to appear to go away. The FTA warrant stays on the books and with the help of modern technology, it is very difficult to slip through the cracks. Newton was just the type of person to take on that challenge.

Newton taunted me by periodically calling me and saying the money would be on its way soon. Yeah, right. This was the ultimate slap in the face, and I think he enjoyed it. He knew damn well that there would never be any money coming my way to cover my losses. I could sense that Newton took pride in Fu*&/n' with me. I don't care what the dictionary definition for evil is because I have my own definition, Newton. He is what evil is and what evil does. This was Newton's way of living. He'd come off as nice person, but would gladly rip my eyes out with a fish hook and drop a deuce in my sockets.

Newton always called from a restricted number, so I couldn't trace the call. Thus, the battle of wits continued. How would I track down this con-artist? I had exhausted all possible leads and basically was down to dumb luck as far as finding him. Even his girlfriend disappeared and most likely joined him on the run. He was a loser, she was a loser, and I certainly was about to be a BIG loser.

Well, the day for me to fork over a large chunk of change arrived and I was physically ill. The six month statutory stay was up and I had to pay the state their forfeiture money. Hey, I knew I would survive, so it wasn't the end of the world for me, BUT I really, really, HATED writing out that check. It still pains me to this day as I write these words. The only satisfaction I could possibly gain from this experience would be seeing Newton locked up in cuffs and leg chains. Then, HE would take my spot as a big loser.

Once the check was written, the only recourse was to sue Newton and/or his cosigner. Well, since they both vanished, I was assed out, as they say.

After I lost the chase and paid the forfeiture money, reports surfaced that Newton was in Cleveland Ohio, or Philadelphia Pennsylvania. Where the hell were these possible leads six months ago? I cared, but not that much about where he was or what he was doing. He got me but good and I didn't want to reopen the wounds caused by paying such a big bond. So I begrudgingly explained to the snitches that all bets were off and it was too late for me to save my skin. Then reports came in that he was back in Connecticut hiding out. Well, if anyone had the cojones to return to his home state, it sure would be Newton. He thought he could "buck" the system. I don't think for one second he had any remorse for his actions. Sociopaths don't feel any guilt; they just inflict pain and misery on others.

About three years after I settled my portion of the case with the state, out of the blue I got a phone call from an officer who had been tracking Newton trying to pick him up for his failure to appear. Newton had been arrested and was finally in custody here in Connecticut. What a great day that was when I found out he had been nabbed. I became an instant psychological winner.

Apparently he had indeed fled the state on the day he was to surrender himself and he had only recently returned. I felt some relief knowing that he hadn't been in close proximity while I was feverishly trying to locate him a few years earlier. That would have been a real tough one to handle, if he had been under my nose all the while.

For all of his cunning and creative criminal endeavors that he had been credited for, the dumb ass slipped up while working as a painter a couple of towns away from where he was well known, and more importantly, wanted for failure to show for a sentencing. The police questioned him on a motor vehicle stop and found out his true identity. He was unceremoniously, and without fanfare, whisked off to an awaiting cinder block jail cell. He was a snake, but now he was a caged snake.

Several years later, I happened to spot Newton shopping at a local Home Depot store. Newton did not see me. I had many nefarious thoughts racing within my cranium. I would have loved to see a lead pipe collide with his head in the area of his medulla oblongata. The instrument was only a couple of aisles away and it was readily available. I also had my choice of pick axes that would have looked good embedded in his skull. I think you get my point. If I had acted out, I would have become just like Newton, a premeditative, calculating, criminal. I cautiously kept my distance and observed the man that caused me to lose a truckload of Ben Franklins. Then I thought to myself, take the high road, leave him be, be professional and practice what you preach.

I made it a point for Newton to see me a few minutes after I contemplated attacking him with a bevy of blunt brain beaters. Our eyes met for only a moment, but it seemed like an eternity. The look I gave Newton was that of an arrow piercing a bulls-eye, dead on ringer, center mass direct hit BINGO!! It had been many years since we had been face to face, but those were much happier times for both of us. He was committing crimes and I was making money off those crimes and convictions.

This meeting was different. When he saw me, he damn near stroked out. His skin tone turned the color of Elmer's Glue and his gait wobbled like the scarecrow on his way to the Emerald City. He bowed his head in obvious shame, which surprised me because he was a sociopath in my opinion, and hurriedly turned his bony bag of flesh away and scooted. Not a word was spoken during this unexpected rendezvous, It was an "in the body experience" for me. As for Newton, I think he got my mental signal loud and clear.

Newton, I'm still waiting for you to reimburse me. After you pay me I will forgive you and as an added bonus, I will waive the ten percent annual interest fee.

Savannah Park

Chapter Eleven
Savannah Park

Sometimes a case comes down to one simple word: LUCK. Luther D. was a quiet, soft spoken, local kid, married with a young son. Luther had trouble keeping a steady job and eventually got caught up in the drug world. He started out small, dealing pot and eventually became a mid-level player on the drug tour. For every successful sale there is a price to pay somewhere down the road. A lowly buyer inevitably gets arrested and then turns on the supplier. This was the exact reason that our paths crossed. Luther was "rolled over on" by a buyer who wanted to save his own skin. Rolling over on a dealer is common in the drug world. Everybody likes the junk but nobody wants to take a pinch, so buyers often sing like canaries. Luther needed to post a substantial bond and called me for my assistance. After some consideration, I decided to take the case and post a $75,000 bond on his behalf. His wife co-signed, and at the time, everything seemed to be in order. Luther made many court appearances, as he was required to do.

When it came down to fight or flight, Luther made like a maiden jumbo jet. Simply stated, Luther disappeared. Not only was he gone, but his wife and child were also gone. I had nothing to back up his bond collateral-wise. Luther had never missed, ever, until this particular case. I think he couldn't face the fact of maybe going to jail and missing out on his young child's formative years. I have to give him credit for not abandoning his wife and young child. I cannot give him credit for leaving me in the lurch for $75,000. So, once again, it was me versus another bail jumper in a game of hide and seek.

People on the streets had no solid leads for me. His players hadn't seen or heard a thing. I really didn't expect much from his crew. They were a tight knit posse and looked out for each other. They all were involved in the drug trade, but Luther was the one that got caught with a fair amount of drugs, and he wasn't about to give up any of his boys, so he took the hit. As crazy as it sounds, that is an admirable characteristic, even if it is for the wrong reason. I finally was able to track down a relative of his in a neighboring town. She had no info for me and was in fact very upset that Luther had taken off with his wife and young son. I must have interrogated her for an hour to pick her brain for any possible lead, but it was all in vain; Luther's relative was of no significant help in my quest for finding him, though she did leak out that Luther might have had family in Harlem, NY. Through internet searches and cross referencing, I was able to get a possible address in Harlem. Harlem would be my next stop in the investigation.

Within a week I was on my way to Harlem with my dear friend Lorenzo. He too, like my brother Garth, was called from this earth too early and without warning. God rest his soul. A true gentle giant, Lorenzo was one of my closest friends and I will always be grateful that he was part of my life. Furthermore, Lorenzo and I often attended Bible Revival conferences, aka football games and Bourbon Street restaurants in New Orleans.

He and I took my car to the Stamford train station and boarded the Metro North express to 125th Street, Harlem. Upon leaving the depot, we walked over to the address of the supposed relative of Luther. Well, let me just say that the address was a bum address. No one ever heard of this so called relative. Lorenzo and I hit a dead end. Dead ends are just another aspect of the investigation process. I needed to keep plugging away, but at that moment, we decided to grab a cab and go into Manhattan for some lunch. Riding in a cab through the streets of New York City was an adventure in and of itself. There are no words to adequately describe how much of a spectacle the concrete jungle streets of New York have to offer. We saw some things that will never leave our memory banks: panhandlers, street merchants, an occasional movie star, freaks and foreigners alike. I must also mention the skyscrapers and the ubiquitous architectural wonders.

Lorenzo and I decided to check out Mulberry St., in little Italy. Once we poured out of the cab near Chinatown, we started to walk up Mulberry St. Some staff members from each restaurant were trying to hawk business and have us dine at their place. The choices seemed endless and the garlicky aroma wafting along the sidewalk was so pungent it could have warded off a horde of vampires. For no particular reason, Lorenzo and I decided on a place called La Mela. Great choice it was. It was a type of restaurant that offered family style dinning as well as a la carte service. Lorenzo and I opted for the family style service and just waited for the unannounced onslaught of delicious food. After a friendly greeting, we were seated, and the bottles of red and white wine were quickly set down on our table in an "I dare you to drink them" fashion. Kinda like the old western movies where the pretty bar maid tempts an unsuspecting tough-guy cowboy to chug laced drinks repeatedly until the bar maid wins the battle and the cowboy is rendered sated and useless. Just like that unwitting cowboy, we had no idea what was in store for us at La Mela. Then arrived the warm and perfectly baked Italian bread. After the delicious bread, dipped in oil and seasonings of course, what next appeared was a tray with about five different appetizers. Right about then we were feeling pretty good about life. The waiter kept a close watch on our table, as well as many others, because with impeccable timing, he plunked down on the table a pasta display that would have made a Roman cry tears of joy. The tortellini, lasagna, manicotti, and linguine were steaming with irresistible aromas. Just when we thought we might have had enough, out came the entrees. Yes, as in plural! Savory pieces of chicken, veal, seafood, steak, and sausage were presented to us as if we were Augustus and Tiberius. Morrone! Gluttonous probably is too soft a word for this dining experience. It didn't matter if the diner waved the "UNCLE" towel, the impishly smirking waiter brought dessert and cappuccino out of the kitchen. We couldn't even look at the waiter because we were disgusted at the thought of ingesting any more food. It didn't matter; he put down the final touches of a monstrous meal next to our over-stuffed gullets. At this point Lorenzo and I were within millimeters of giving them back most of their food by way of the old "index finger down the throat" magic trick. I think you get the picture.

When we finally did leave the restaurant, it felt like we had escaped! We then cabbed it to Grand Central, and made our way back to Connecticut. Hey, even when we were out on a mission, we had to sustain ourselves. This was definitely overkill, but an unforgettable, unusual experience. I have since been back to La Mela, but I have managed to eat their fabulous food in moderation.

As the weeks passed, Luther was still at large. I exhausted all possible leads and trails to follow. Where the hell could this guy be? More often than not, bail jumpers return sooner or later. Luther was pretty good at this hiding game and I was slowly bracing myself for the distinct possibility of paying his bond forfeiture. The six months were going to expire in Mid-October and I only had a couple of weeks left.

I told my family that if Luther got caught, then I would put a swimming pool in our backyard. I had been saving the money to pay the bond, so I figured I would put it to good use. Growing up I envied our neighbors with swimming pools. All we had was a hose. What kind of fun was that? I suppose it's better than no hose.

A week before the money was due, I petitioned the State's Attorney for an extension of time. I explained that I was doing everything under my power to try to get this kid back. (I didn't mention La Mela's restaurant.) The State's Attorney was kind enough to grant me more time. I had a final deadline of New Year's Eve. I called upon another good friend, Sunny, who had some fantastic connections. Thanks to my friend, federal authorities were aware of this guy and took some interest in tracking him. Being on the run with a small child usually strikes a chord with law enforcement. No one wants to see a child in the middle of a mess such as this mess. I felt some relief that now more agencies were trying to get him. I had a lot of help in my quest for Luther; local, state, and federal authorities were involved.

As I said in the beginning of this chapter, LUCK was the key word. I received a call from my friend Sunny on or about December 29, two days shy of New Year's Eve. She advised me that Luther was in custody in Savannah, GA. Thank the heavens!! I had two days to spare. Luck was on my side for sure. Evidently, his wife had used a credit card in the Savannah area. The feds had tracked them down relatively soon after learning about Luther, but it took some time to pinpoint their whereabouts. When Luther was ripe for picking, the semi grim reaper took him down. Man, was I happy to hear he was in the bag and would be back up in Connecticut within a few days.

The following day I notified the court and the State's Attorney's office that Luther was in custody in Georgia. I really didn't have any proof other than the phone call, but I assured them that he was indeed captured. Luther finally made it back to the local police station, the same place where I had posted his bail bond. I was granted an interview with him down in the booking room. We talked for a few minutes, and Luther must have apologized twenty times in that time frame. He was truly sorry, and he felt guilty for putting me through such a tension filled eight months. I didn't ask him if I was close to getting him at any point because it didn't matter. He was incarcerated, and I was released from the bond.

Closure to this case was a great end of the year present. A few weeks later I hosted a party at a local restaurant. It was a celebration of sorts and also a thank you gesture on my part. I invited a few of the key players in Luther's apprehension. Every attendee was on a full scholarship plan bankrolled by yours truly. We had a raucous time, but I was a bit disappointed in the tab. To tell you the truth, I thought the bill would be much higher considering some of the sots I invited.

Near the end of spring, the trucks arrived to start on the gift I promised my family. The swimming pool became a reality. As you know I have nicknames for just about everything and everyone. My back yard oasis is officially called Savannah Park. Each summer I often reminisce poolside about how all the crazy twists and turns that this case, and countless others, has affected my very existence. As I've mentioned many times, bail bonds is not my career, it is my way of life. It's just a matter of time before I'm off on another manhunt, so I can't get too complacent.

Today I am joined in the business by my two sons. My youngest child, my daughter, I am keeping away from this grimy business. After thirty years in the bail industry I still hear some creative excuses and twisted stories from some of my clients. As each new day dawns, I greet it with the same question: Who will be the next player in this real life game of hide and seek?

Acknowledgements

I'd like to acknowledge and thank Patricia Zajac for her dedication on this project and her efforts in editing. Secondly, I'd like to thank Eddie "Spaghetti" Siebert, for his guidance and advisement on this project. Finally, thanks to Nussa Kraem, for her artistic prowess.

A note from the author

I hope you enjoyed this book as much as I did penning it. Only time separates me from more bail jumping capers. I hope to have a second edition soon with more wins and losses in the bail industry game of hide and seek.

To order more copies of Bail Guy Prose and Convicts please visit us @:

www.createspace.com/4392812

www.bailguymerchandise.storenvy.com

www.biestekbailbonds.com

Made in the USA
Middletown, DE
15 April 2016